ASVAB

Math Workbook

**Essential Learning Math Skills
Plus Two Complete ASVAB
Math Practice Tests**

By

Michael Smith & Reza Nazari

ASVAB Math Workbook

Published in the United State of America By

The Math Notion

Web: WWW.MathNotion.Com

Email: info@Mathnotion.com

About the Author

Michael Smith has been a math instructor for over a decade now. He holds a master's degree in Management. Since 2006, Michael has devoted his time to both teaching and developing exceptional math learning materials. As a Math instructor and test prep expert, Michael has worked with thousands of students. He has used the feedback of his students to develop a unique study program that can be used by students to drastically improve their math score fast and effectively.

– **AFOQT Math Practice Book**

– **OAR Math Practice Book**

– **GED Math Practice Book**

– **HiSET Math Practice Book**

– **TASC Math Practice Book**

–**many Math Education Workbooks, Exercise Books and Study Guides**

As an experienced Math teacher, Mr. Smith employs a variety of formats to help students achieve their goals: He tutors online and in person, he teaches students in large groups, and he provides training materials and textbooks through his website and through Amazon.

You can contact Michael via email at:

info@Mathnotion.com

Prepare for The ASVAB Math Test with a Perfect Workbook!

ASVAB Math Workbook is a learning workbook to prevent learning loss. It helps you retain and strengthen your Math skills and provides a strong foundation for success. This ASVAB book provides you with solid foundation to get a head starts on your upcoming ASVAB Test.

ASVAB Math Workbook is designed by top ASVAB test prep experts to help students prepare for the ASVAB math questions. It provides test-takers with an in-depth focus on the math section of the test, helping them master the essential math skills that test-takers find the most troublesome. This is a prestigious resource for those who need an extra practice to succeed on the ASVAB Math test.

ASVAB Math Workbook contains many exciting and unique features to help you score higher on the ASVAB Math test, including:

- Over 2,500 ASVAB Math Practice questions with answers
- Complete coverage of all Math concepts which students will need to ace the ASVAB test
- Content 100% aligned with the latest ASVAB test
- Written by ASVAB Math experts
- 2 full-length ASVAB Math practice tests (featuring new question types) with detailed answers

This Comprehensive Workbook for the ASVAB Math lessons is a perfect resource for those ASVAB Math test takers who want to review core content areas, brush-up in math, discover their strengths and weaknesses, and achieve their best scores on the ASVAB test.

WWW.MathNotion.COM

… So Much More Online!

✓ FREE Math Lessons

✓ More Math Learning Books!

✓ Mathematics Worksheets

✓ Online Math Tutors

For a PDF Version of This Book

Please Visit WWW.MathNotion.com

contents

Chapter 1:

Integers and Number Theory

Topics that you will practice in this chapter:

- ✓ Rounding
- ✓ Whole Number Addition and Subtraction
- ✓ Whole Number Multiplication and Division
- ✓ Rounding and Estimates
- ✓ Adding and Subtracting Integers
- ✓ Multiplying and Dividing Integers
- ✓ Order of Operations
- ✓ Ordering Integers and Numbers
- ✓ Integers and Absolute Value
- ✓ Factoring Numbers
- ✓ Greatest Common Factor (GCF)
- ✓ Least Common Multiple (LCM)

"Wherever there is number, there is beauty." −*Proclus*

Rounding

✎ **Round each number to the nearest ten.**

1) 52 = ___   5) 42 = ___   9) 48 = ___

2) 89 = ___   6) 78 = ___   10) 21 = ___

3) 34 = ___   7) 121 = ___   11) 134 = ___

4) 66 = ___   8) 91 = ___   12) 157 = ___

✎ **Round each number to the nearest hundred.**

13) 148 = ___   17) 522 = ___   21) 780 = ___

14) 368 = ___   18) 169 = ___   22) 833 = ___

15) 619 = ___   19) 491 = ___   23) 498 = ___

16) 194 = ___   20) 717 = ___   24) 947 = ___

✎ **Round each number to the nearest thousand.**

25) 3,325 = ___   29) 6,075 = ___   33) 75,952 = ___

26) 2,598 = ___   30) 36,893 = ___   34) 95,250 = ___

27) 4,099 = ___   31) 52,199 = ___   35) 78,680 = ___

28) 5,808 = ___   32) 80,958 = ___   36) 97,869 = ___

Whole Number Addition and Subtraction

✎ **Find the sum or subtract.**

1)
$$
\begin{array}{r}
1,982 \\
+\ 895 \\
\hline
\end{array}
$$

5)
$$
\begin{array}{r}
1,125 \\
+\ 859.35 \\
\hline
\end{array}
$$

9)
$$
\begin{array}{r}
7,322 \\
-\ 895.9 \\
\hline
\end{array}
$$

2)
$$
\begin{array}{r}
3,658 \\
-\ 1,254 \\
\hline
\end{array}
$$

6)
$$
\begin{array}{r}
857.26 \\
+989.15 \\
\hline
\end{array}
$$

10)
$$
\begin{array}{r}
8,921.45 \\
-\ 5,214.25 \\
\hline
\end{array}
$$

3)
$$
\begin{array}{r}
582.54 \\
-\ 321.45 \\
\hline
\end{array}
$$

7)
$$
\begin{array}{r}
254.35 \\
+123.89 \\
\hline
\end{array}
$$

11)
$$
\begin{array}{r}
2,321.25 \\
+\ 1,984.99 \\
\hline
\end{array}
$$

4)
$$
\begin{array}{r}
1,254 \\
+\ 852.98 \\
\hline
\end{array}
$$

8)
$$
\begin{array}{r}
3,257.5 \\
+1,245.2 \\
\hline
\end{array}
$$

12)
$$
\begin{array}{r}
9,914.09 \\
-6,621.12 \\
\hline
\end{array}
$$

✎ **Find the missing number.**

13) $362.5 + \underline{\quad} = 985.3$

16) $2,785 - 1,234.12 = \underline{\quad}$

14) $3,856 - \underline{\quad} = 2,009.5$

17) $999.9 + \underline{\quad} = 1,234.6$

15) $\underline{\quad} - 985.1 = 1,450.9$

18) $5,758.8 - 3,758.85 = \underline{\quad}$

Whole Number Multiplication and Division

✎ **Calculate each product.**

1) $\begin{array}{r} 35 \\ \times\ 43 \\ \hline \end{array}$

3) $\begin{array}{r} 37.2 \\ \times\ 16 \\ \hline \end{array}$

5) $\begin{array}{r} 158.8 \\ \times\ 15.4 \\ \hline \end{array}$

2) $\begin{array}{r} 53.2 \\ \times\ 12.5 \\ \hline \end{array}$

4) $\begin{array}{r} 27.5 \\ \times 26 \\ \hline \end{array}$

6) $\begin{array}{r} 143.2 \\ \times\ 15.5 \\ \hline \end{array}$

✎ **Find the missing quotient.**

7) $600 \div 1.5 = $ _____

8) $780 \div 39 = $ _____

9) $390 \div 1.3 = $ _____

10) $900 \div 0.9 = $ _____

11) $156 \div 40 = $ _____

12) $112 \div 1.6 = $ _____

13) $660 \div 2.2 = $ _____

14) $400 \div 0.8 = $ _____

15) $2{,}040 \div 25.5 = $ _____

16) $9{,}360 \div 31.2 = $ _____

✎ **Calculate each problem.**

17) $560 \div 7 = N,\ N = $ ___

18) $315 \div 4.5 = N,\ N = $ ___

19) $N \div 9 = 65,\ N = $ ___

20) $24.6 \times N = 147.6,\ N = $ ___

21) $985 \div N = 1{,}970,\ N = $ ___

22) $N \times 3.5 = 147,\ N = $ ___

Rounding and Estimates

✍ **Estimate the sum by rounding each number to the nearest ten.**

1) $19 + 23 =$ _____

2) $72 + 31 =$ _____

3) $48 + 63 =$ _____

4) $44 + 86 =$ _____

5) $169 + 212 =$ _____

6) $650 + 323 =$ _____

7) $598 + 575 =$ _____

8) $1,586 + 3,355 =$ _____

✍ **Estimate the product by rounding each number to the nearest ten.**

9) $37 \times 43 =$ _____

10) $12 \times 31 =$ _____

11) $48 \times 54 =$ _____

12) $17 \times 33 =$ _____

13) $68 \times 27 =$ _____

14) $91 \times 21 =$ _____

15) $86 \times 37 =$ _____

16) $96 \times 42 =$ _____

✍ **Estimate the sum or product by rounding each number to the nearest ten.**

17) $\begin{array}{r} 28 \\ \times\ 16 \\ \hline \end{array}$

18) $\begin{array}{r} 72 \\ \times\ 22 \\ \hline \end{array}$

19) $\begin{array}{r} 85 \\ +\ 64 \\ \hline \end{array}$

20) $\begin{array}{r} 43 \\ +91 \\ \hline \end{array}$

21) $\begin{array}{r} 64 \\ \times\ 39 \\ \hline \end{array}$

22) $\begin{array}{r} 99 \\ +\ 54 \\ \hline \end{array}$

Adding and Subtracting Integers

✎ **Find each sum.**

1) $15 + (-35) =$

2) $(-28) + (-29) =$

3) $19 + (-27) =$

4) $57 + (-64) =$

5) $(-14) + (-19) + 64 =$

6) $54 + (-36) + 19 =$

7) $46 + (-30) + (-33) + 29 =$

8) $(-40) + (-70) + 28 + 55 =$

9) $60 + (-65) + (83 - 72) =$

10) $49 + (-55) + (90 - 67) =$

✎ **Find each difference.**

11) $(-32) - (-7) =$

12) $40 - (-12) =$

13) $(-60) - 56 =$

14) $27 - (-17) =$

15) $58 - (76 - 29) =$

16) $19 - (-14) - (-22) =$

17) $(39 + 15) - (-46) =$

18) $49 - 17 - (-13) =$

19) $85 - 45 - (-18) =$

20) $78 - (-35) - (-63) =$

21) $89 - (-11) - (-26) =$

22) $(19 - 50) - (-95) =$

23) $46 - 49 - (-87) =$

24) $120 - (98 + 24) - (-38) =$

25) $112 - (-102) + (-81) =$

26) $108 - (-42) + (-89) =$

Multiplying and Dividing Integers

✍ **Find each product.**

1) $(-7) \times (-9) =$

2) $(-5) \times 6 =$

3) $10 \times (-15) =$

4) $(-9) \times (-25) =$

5) $(-7) \times (-12) \times 13 =$

6) $(15 - 4) \times (-11) =$

7) $25 \times (-4) \times (-5) =$

8) $(85 + 10) \times (-11) =$

9) $12 \times (-19 + 12) \times 5 =$

10) $(-15) \times (-18) \times (-20) =$

✍ **Find each quotient.**

11) $85 \div (-5) =$

12) $(-90) \div (-15) =$

13) $(-121) \div (-11) =$

14) $99 \div (-33) =$

15) $(-114) \div 2 =$

16) $(-208) \div (-16) =$

17) $198 \div (-11) =$

18) $(-364) \div (-14) =$

19) $255 \div (-15) =$

20) $(-378) \div (18) =$

21) $(-184) \div (-8) =$

22) $-437 \div (-23) =$

23) $(-570) \div (-19) =$

24) $480 \div (-32) =$

25) $(-546) \div (-21) =$

26) $(486) \div (-54) =$

Order of Operations

✎ **Evaluate each expression.**

1) $7 + (5 \times 8) =$

2) $16 - (6 \times 9) =$

3) $(17 \times 5) + 12 =$

4) $(24 - 12) - (11 \times 4) =$

5) $35 + (18 \div 3) =$

6) $(27 \times 3) \div 3 =$

7) $(88 \div 4) \times (-5) =$

8) $(9 \times 9) + (86 - 52) =$

9) $78 + (5 \times 12) + 14 =$

10) $(60 \times 4) \div (4 + 2) =$

11) $(-15) + (14 \times 4) + 18 =$

12) $(14 \times 5) - (56 \div 7) =$

13) $(7 \times 9 \div 3) - (32 + 21) =$

14) $(45 + 11 - 14) \times 2 - 15 =$

15) $(40 - 18 + 20) \times (75 \div 3) =$

16) $75 + \big(54 - (45 \div 9)\big) =$

17) $(12 + 15 - 24) + (44 \div 4) =$

18) $(78 - 19) + (27 - 10 + 7) =$

19) $(18 \times 3) + (17 \times 9) - 52 =$

20) $65 + 17 - (45 \times 2) + 40 =$

Ordering Integers and Numbers

✍ **Order each set of integers from least to greatest.**

1) $17, -15, -8, 0, 9$ ___, ___, ___, ___, ___, ___

2) $-14, -26, 17, 42, 39$ ___, ___, ___, ___, ___, ___

3) $32, -15, -69, 41, -80$ ___, ___, ___, ___, ___, ___

4) $-49, -65, 35, -21, 68$ ___, ___, ___, ___, ___, ___

5) $69, -32, 10, -45, 24$ ___, ___, ___, ___, ___, ___

6) $108, 76, -59, 87, -78$ ___, ___, ___, ___, ___, ___

✍ **Order each set of integers from greatest to least.**

7) $62, 98, -7, -19, -1$ ___, ___, ___, ___, ___, ___

8) $34, 35, -24, -46, 56$ ___, ___, ___, ___, ___, ___

9) $35, -96, -58, 17, -34$ ___, ___, ___, ___, ___, ___

10) $37, 12, -26, -13, 52$ ___, ___, ___, ___, ___, ___

11) $-12, 66, -18, -28, 54$ ___, ___, ___, ___, ___, ___

12) $-100, -85, -30, 5, 9$ ___, ___, ___, ___, ___, ___

Integers and Absolute Value

✍ **Write absolute value of each number.**

1) $|-19| =$

2) $|-32| =$

3) $|-50| =$

4) $|31| =$

5) $|57| =$

6) $|-76| =$

7) $|42| =$

8) $|101| =$

9) $|28| =$

10) $|-49| =$

11) $|-13|$

12) $|78| =$

13) $|100| =$

14) $|0| =$

15) $|-105| =$

16) $|-77| =$

17) $88 =$

18) $|-29| =$

19) $|112| =$

20) $|-120| =$

✍ **Evaluate the value.**

21) $|-5| - \frac{|-40|}{8} =$

22) $18 - |4 - 19| - |-15| =$

23) $\frac{|-72|}{9} \times |-9| =$

24) $\frac{|6 \times (-8)|}{3} \times \frac{|-21|}{7} =$

25) $|5 \times (-9)| + \frac{|-110|}{11} =$

26) $\frac{|-96|}{12} \times \frac{|-27|}{9} =$

27) $|-19 + 12| \times \frac{|-12 \times 13|}{7} =$

28) $\frac{|-19 \times 6|}{3} \times |-11| =$

Factoring Numbers

✎ **List all positive factors of each number.**

1) 6

2) 21

3) 28

4) 26

5) 46

6) 45

7) 48

8) 50

9) 52

10) 63

11) 70

12) 72

13) 78

14) 80

15) 82

16) 88

17) 90

18) 93

19) 95

20) 96

21) 98

22) 102

23) 124

24) 125

Greatest Common Factor

✎ **Find the GCF for each number pair.**

1) 6, 2	9) 9, 15	17) 28, 21
2) 8, 4	10) 4, 18	18) 56, 72
3) 5, 3	11) 14, 18	19) 34, 51
4) 6, 4	12) 25, 30	20) 6, 18, 27
5) 7, 5	13) 27, 45	21) 2, 9, 8
6) 8, 18	14) 36, 18	22) 10, 12, 24
7) 14, 21	15) 9, 12	23) 5, 14, 21
8) 6, 14	16) 11, 8	24) 72, 9, 18

Least Common Multiple

✎ **Find the LCM for each number pair.**

1) 6, 5

2) 8, 18

3) 9, 15

4) 15, 20

5) 20, 25

6) 22, 33

7) 6, 28

8) 8, 14

9) 21, 28

10) 14, 28

11) 9, 30

12) 7, 12

13) 12, 36

14) 9, 54

15) 42, 21

16) 40, 16

17) 12, 42

18) 13, 11

19) 32, 72

20) 15, 27

21) 24, 44

22) 8, 12, 42

23) 2, 6, 11

24) 15, 25, 30

Answers of Worksheets – Chapter 1

Rounding

1) 50	10) 20	19) 500	28) 6,000
2) 90	11) 130	20) 700	29) 6,000
3) 30	12) 160	21) 800	30) 37,000
4) 70	13) 100	22) 800	31) 52,000
5) 40	14) 400	23) 500	32) 81,000
6) 80	15) 600	24) 900	33) 76,000
7) 120	16) 200	25) 3,000	34) 95,000
8) 90	17) 500	26) 3,000	35) 79,000
9) 50	18) 200	27) 4,000	36) 98,000

Whole Number Addition and Subtraction

1) 2,877	7) 378.24	13) 622.8
2) 2,404	8) 4,502.7	14) 1,846.5
3) 261.09	9) 6,426.1	15) 2,436
4) 2,106.98	10) 3,707.2	16) 1,550.88
5) 1,984.35	11) 4,306.24	17) 234.7
6) 1,846.41	12) 3,292.97	18) 1,999.95

Whole Number Multiplication and Division

1) 1,505	7) 400	13) 300	19) 585
2) 665	8) 20	14) 500	20) 6
3) 595.2	9) 300	15) 80	21) 2
4) 715	10) 1,000	16) 300	22) 42
5) 2,445.52	11) 3.9	17) 80	
6) 2,219.6	12) 70	18) 70	

Rounding and Estimates

1) 40	6) 970	11) 2,500	16) 4,200
2) 100	7) 1,180	12) 600	17) 600
3) 110	8) 4,950	13) 2,100	18) 1,400
4) 130	9) 1,600	14) 1,800	19) 150
5) 380	10) 300	15) 3,600	20) 130

21) 2,400   22) 150

Adding and Subtracting Integers

1) −20	8) −27	15) 11	22) 64
2) −57	9) 6	16) 55	23) 84
3) −8	10) 17	17) 100	24) 36
4) −7	11) −25	18) 45	25) 133
5) 31	12) 52	19) 58	26) 61
6) 37	13) −116	20) 176	
7) 12	14) 44	21) 126	

Multiplying and Dividing Integers

1) 63	8) −1,045	15) −57	22) 19
2) −30	9) −420	16) 13	23) 30
3) −150	10) −5,400	17) −18	24) −15
4) 225	11) −17	18) 26	25) 26
5) 1,092	12) 6	19) −17	26) −9
6) −121	13) 11	20) −21	
7) 500	14) −3	21) 23	

Order of Operations

1) 47	6) 27	11) 59	16) 124
2) −38	7) −110	12) 62	17) 14
3) 97	8) 115	13) −32	18) 83
4) −32	9) 152	14) 69	19) 155
5) 41	10) 40	15) 1,050	20) 32

Ordering Integers and Numbers

1) −15, −8, 0, 9, 17	7) 98, 62, −1, −7, −19
2) −26, −14, 17, 39, 42	8) 56, 35, 34, −24, −46
3) −80, −69, −15, 32, 41	9) 35, 17, −34, −58, −96
4) −65, −49, −21, 35, 68	10) 52, 37, 12, −13, −26
5) −45, −32, 10, 24, 69	11) 66, 54, −12, −18, −28
6) −78, −59, 76, 87, 108	12) 9, 5, −30, −85, −100

Integers and Absolute Value

1) 19	8) 101	15) 105	22) -12
2) 32	9) 28	16) 77	23) 72
3) 50	10) 49	17) 88	24) 48
4) 31	11) 13	18) 29	25) 55
5) 57	12) 78	19) 112	26) 24
6) 76	13) 100	20) 120	27) 156
7) 42	14) 0	21) 0	28) 418

Factoring Numbers

1) 1, 2, 3, 6

2) 1, 3, 7, 21

3) 1, 2, 4, 7, 14, 28

4) 1, 2, 13, 26

5) 1, 2, 23, 46

6) 1, 3, 5, 9, 15, 45

7) 1, 2, 3, 4, 6, 8, 12, 16, 24, 48

8) 1, 2, 5, 10, 25, 50

9) 1, 2, 4, 5, 13, 26, 52

10) 1, 3, 7, 9, 21, 63

11) 1, 2, 5, 7, 10, 14, 35, 70

12) 1, 2, 3, 4, 6, 8, 9, 12, 18 24, 36, 72

13) 1, 2, 3, 6, 13, 26, 39, 78

14) 1, 2, 4, 5, 8, 10, 16, 20, 40, 80

15) 1, 2, 41, 82

16) 1, 2, 4, 8, 11, 22, 44, 88

17) 1, 2, 3, 5, 6, 9, 10, 15, 18, 30, 45, 90

18) 1, 3, 31, 93

19) 1, 5, 19, 95

20) 1, 2, 3, 4, 6, 8, 12, 16, 24, 32, 48, 96

21) 1, 2, 7, 14, 49, 98

22) 1, 2, 3, 6, 17, 34, 51, 102

23) 1, 2, 4, 31, 62, 124

24) 1, 5, 25, 125

Greatest Common Factor

1) 2	7) 7	13) 9	19) 17
2) 4	8) 2	14) 18	20) 3
3) 1	9) 3	15) 3	21) 1
4) 2	10) 2	16) 1	22) 2
5) 1	11) 2	17) 7	23) 1
6) 2	12) 5	18) 8	24) 9

Least Common Multiple

1) 30	7) 84	13) 36	19) 288
2) 72	8) 56	14) 54	20) 135
3) 45	9) 84	15) 42	21) 264
4) 60	10) 28	16) 80	22) 168
5) 100	11) 90	17) 84	23) 66
6) 66	12) 84	18) 143	24) 150

Chapter 2:

Fractions and Decimals

Topics that you will practice in this chapter:

- ✓ Simplifying Fractions
- ✓ Adding and Subtracting Fractions
- ✓ Multiplying and Dividing Fractions
- ✓ Adding and Subtract Mixed Numbers
- ✓ Multiplying and
- Dividing Mixed Numbers
- ✓ Adding and Subtracting Decimals
- ✓ Multiplying and Dividing Decimals
- ✓ Comparing Decimals
- ✓ Rounding Decimals

"A Man is like a fraction whose numerator is what he is and whose denominator is what he thinks of himself. The larger the denominator, the smaller the fraction." –Tolstoy

Simplifying Fractions

✎ **Simplify each fraction to its lowest terms.**

1) $\frac{8}{16} =$

2) $\frac{28}{35} =$

3) $\frac{27}{36} =$

4) $\frac{70}{140} =$

5) $\frac{13}{52} =$

6) $\frac{38}{57} =$

7) $\frac{64}{80} =$

8) $\frac{21}{84} =$

9) $\frac{85}{170} =$

10) $\frac{120}{168} =$

11) $\frac{31}{124} =$

12) $\frac{48}{96} =$

13) $\frac{98}{112} =$

14) $\frac{99}{110} =$

15) $\frac{51}{153} =$

16) $\frac{40}{112} =$

17) $\frac{90}{225} =$

18) $\frac{44}{297} =$

19) $\frac{54}{279} =$

20) $\frac{320}{720} =$

21) $\frac{70}{560} =$

✎ **Find the answer for each problem.**

22) Which of the following fractions equal to $\frac{3}{7}$? _____

    A. $\frac{24}{63}$ B. $\frac{51}{109}$ C. $\frac{51}{119}$ D. $\frac{240}{630}$

23) Which of the following fractions equal to $\frac{7}{8}$? _____

    A. $\frac{182}{208}$ B. $\frac{175}{208}$ C. $\frac{182}{216}$ D. $\frac{49}{64}$

24) Which of the following fractions equal to $\frac{2}{9}$? _____

    A. $\frac{64}{126}$ B. $\frac{46}{207}$ C. $\frac{48}{207}$ D. $\frac{56}{208}$

Adding and Subtracting Fractions

✍ Find the sum.

1) $\dfrac{5x}{8} + \dfrac{3x}{8} =$

2) $\dfrac{x}{2} + \dfrac{x}{7} =$

3) $\dfrac{y}{3} + \dfrac{y}{4} =$

4) $\dfrac{3x}{8} + \dfrac{2x}{5} =$

5) $\dfrac{xy}{5} + \dfrac{2xy}{7} =$

6) $\dfrac{2x}{9} + \dfrac{4x}{9} =$

7) $\dfrac{a}{4} + \dfrac{2a}{3} =$

8) $\dfrac{2}{x} + \dfrac{4}{x} =$

9) $\dfrac{1}{a} + \dfrac{2}{b} =$

10) $\dfrac{3b}{5} + \dfrac{2b}{7} =$

11) $\dfrac{a}{y} + \dfrac{3a}{y} =$

12) $\dfrac{3}{x} + \dfrac{1}{2x} =$

✍ Find the difference.

13) $\dfrac{x}{3} - \dfrac{x}{6} =$

14) $\dfrac{2x}{5} - \dfrac{3x}{8} =$

15) $\dfrac{x}{7} - \dfrac{y}{7} =$

16) $\dfrac{2x}{7} - \dfrac{x}{6} =$

17) $\dfrac{5a}{9} - \dfrac{2a}{5} =$

18) $\dfrac{2ab}{3} - \dfrac{ab}{6} =$

19) $\dfrac{1}{x} - \dfrac{1}{3x} =$

20) $\dfrac{4}{y} - \dfrac{3}{4y} =$

21) $\dfrac{5}{x} - \dfrac{2y}{xy} =$

22) $\dfrac{8}{ab} - \dfrac{5}{3ab} =$

23) $\dfrac{2a}{y} - \dfrac{a}{3y} =$

24) $\dfrac{5}{b} - \dfrac{2}{3b} =$

25) $\dfrac{2a}{b} - \dfrac{a}{b} =$

26) $\dfrac{3}{a} - \dfrac{2}{b} =$

27) $\dfrac{4a}{b} - \dfrac{2a}{3b} =$

28) $\dfrac{6}{xy} - \dfrac{7}{2xy} =$

29) $\dfrac{2}{a} - \dfrac{1}{4a} =$

30) $\dfrac{2a}{3b} - \dfrac{4a}{9b} =$

Multiplying and Dividing Fractions

✎ Find the value of each expression in lowest terms.

1) $\frac{3}{a} \times \frac{5}{3} =$

2) $\frac{2}{3b} \times \frac{9}{2} =$

3) $\frac{a}{15} \times \frac{5}{2a} =$

4) $\frac{x}{3a} \times \frac{9a}{6x} =$

5) $\frac{x}{12} \times \frac{6}{y} =$

6) $\frac{7}{x} \times \frac{x}{14} =$

7) $\frac{10}{3a} \times \frac{6}{20} =$

8) $\frac{4a}{b} \times \frac{2b}{5} =$

9) $\frac{2ab}{7} \times \frac{14}{6ab} =$

10) $\frac{4a}{5b} \times \frac{15}{2a} =$

11) $\frac{ab}{21} \times \frac{7}{a} =$

12) $\frac{a}{cd} \times \frac{2bc}{a} =$

✎ Find the value of each expression in lowest terms.

13) $\frac{a}{2} \div \frac{a}{4} =$

14) $\frac{b}{3} \div \frac{b}{9} =$

15) $\frac{a}{b} \div \frac{3}{b} =$

16) $\frac{2a}{15} \div \frac{4a}{5} =$

17) $\frac{1}{a} \div \frac{b}{3a} =$

18) $\frac{4a}{3b} \div \frac{a}{2b} =$

19) $\frac{a}{8} \div \frac{3a}{16} =$

20) $\frac{3b}{20} \div \frac{6b}{15a} =$

21) $\frac{x}{12y} \div \frac{2x}{9y} =$

22) $\frac{25}{x} \div \frac{50}{2x} =$

23) $\frac{16}{5ab} \div \frac{32}{ab} =$

24) $\frac{7a}{b} \div \frac{8a}{b} =$

25) $\frac{5}{x} \div \frac{3y}{x} =$

26) $\frac{2a}{21} \div \frac{a}{14} =$

27) $\frac{ab}{x} \div \frac{a}{x} =$

28) $\frac{6}{a} \div \frac{3b}{2a} =$

29) $\frac{9}{16a} \div \frac{3}{8ab} =$

30) $\frac{24}{xy} \div \frac{12}{y} =$

Adding and Subtracting Mixed Numbers

✍ **Find the sum.**

1) $3\frac{5}{6} + 2\frac{1}{3} =$

2) $4\frac{2}{5} + 1\frac{1}{5} =$

3) $5\frac{1}{8} + 6\frac{3}{4} =$

4) $2\frac{2}{3} + 3\frac{1}{2} =$

5) $3\frac{4}{5} + 3\frac{2}{15} =$

6) $8\frac{1}{16} + 3\frac{3}{8} =$

7) $4\frac{3}{5} + 4\frac{1}{6} =$

8) $7\frac{3}{4} + 3\frac{5}{6} =$

9) $8\frac{5}{6} + 2\frac{2}{7} =$

10) $11\frac{3}{16} + 3\frac{5}{24} =$

✍ **Find the difference.**

11) $3\frac{3}{4} - 2\frac{1}{4} =$

12) $5\frac{1}{7} - 3\frac{1}{7} =$

13) $4\frac{1}{3} - 1\frac{1}{9} =$

14) $7\frac{1}{6} - 3\frac{1}{12} =$

15) $6\frac{1}{3} - 2\frac{5}{18} =$

16) $8\frac{1}{4} - 5\frac{1}{8} =$

17) $9\frac{1}{2} - 6\frac{1}{5} =$

18) $11\frac{7}{15} - 8\frac{1}{30} =$

19) $12\frac{3}{5} - 7\frac{2}{7} =$

20) $18\frac{1}{8} - 14\frac{3}{16} =$

21) $12\frac{2}{3} - 11\frac{7}{15} =$

22) $3\frac{1}{5} - 1\frac{1}{2} =$

23) $14\frac{3}{5} - 6\frac{4}{5} =$

24) $17\frac{1}{4} - 14\frac{8}{9} =$

25) $24\frac{3}{9} - 15\frac{1}{18} =$

26) $28\frac{3}{7} - 19\frac{5}{6} =$

Multiplying and Dividing Mixed Numbers

✎ **Find the product.**

1) $2\frac{1}{3} \times 4\frac{1}{2} =$

2) $4\frac{1}{5} \times 2\frac{1}{3} =$

3) $7\frac{2}{3} \times 3\frac{3}{5} =$

4) $9\frac{2}{7} \times 3\frac{1}{8} =$

5) $5\frac{4}{11} \times 4\frac{1}{3} =$

6) $7\frac{3}{8} \times 5\frac{4}{9} =$

7) $9\frac{2}{3} \times 11\frac{5}{6} =$

8) $8\frac{3}{5} \times 7\frac{4}{9} =$

9) $5\frac{1}{9} \times 9\frac{5}{8} =$

10) $10\frac{2}{7} \times 2\frac{5}{8} =$

✎ **Find the quotient.**

11) $2\frac{1}{8} \div 1\frac{3}{8} =$

12) $4\frac{1}{6} \div 2\frac{1}{3} =$

13) $7\frac{1}{3} \div 3\frac{3}{4} =$

14) $4\frac{5}{8} \div 1\frac{1}{2} =$

15) $6\frac{5}{12} \div 4\frac{1}{6} =$

16) $5\frac{7}{18} \div 5\frac{1}{6} =$

17) $6\frac{5}{21} \div 2\frac{3}{7} =$

18) $8\frac{1}{7} \div 8\frac{1}{14} =$

19) $10\frac{1}{4} \div 3\frac{2}{5} =$

20) $15\frac{1}{3} \div 5\frac{2}{9} =$

21) $12\frac{1}{3} \div 6\frac{1}{2} =$

22) $18\frac{1}{9} \div 18\frac{1}{6} =$

23) $10\frac{3}{4} \div 5\frac{2}{5} =$

24) $11\frac{1}{3} \div 8\frac{4}{5} =$

25) $9\frac{1}{6} \div 3\frac{2}{7} =$

26) $7\frac{1}{3} \div 3\frac{7}{11} =$

Adding and Subtracting Decimals

✍ **Add and subtract decimals.**

1)
$$\begin{array}{r} 52.18 \\ -\ 21.27 \\ \hline \end{array}$$

4)
$$\begin{array}{r} 65.84 \\ -\ 35.49 \\ \hline \end{array}$$

7)
$$\begin{array}{r} 98.12 \\ -\ 45.55 \\ \hline \end{array}$$

2)
$$\begin{array}{r} 49.34 \\ +\ 25.24 \\ \hline \end{array}$$

5)
$$\begin{array}{r} 54.57 \\ +\ 18.37 \\ \hline \end{array}$$

8)
$$\begin{array}{r} 48.99 \\ +\ 57.67 \\ \hline \end{array}$$

3)
$$\begin{array}{r} 48.60 \\ +\ 35.75 \\ \hline \end{array}$$

6)
$$\begin{array}{r} 90.45 \\ -\ 28.75 \\ \hline \end{array}$$

9)
$$\begin{array}{r} 158.05 \\ -\ 78.98 \\ \hline \end{array}$$

✍ **Find the missing number.**

10) ___ $+ 4.9 = 6.5$

15) ___ $- 19.98 = 8.17$

11) $5.15 +$ ___ $= 6.43$

16) $38.89 +$ ___ $= 41.32$

12) $8.09 +$ ___ $= 11.84$

17) ___ $- 35.99 = 1.80$

13) $8.88 -$ ___ $= 6.78$

18) ___ $+ 39.08 = 41.36$

14) ___ $- 1.59 = 3.71$

19) $98.98 +$ ___ $= 123.68$

Multiplying and Dividing Decimals

✎ **Find the product.**

1) $0.6 \times 0.8 =$

2) $2.5 \times 0.9 =$

3) $0.87 \times 0.4 =$

4) $0.15 \times 0.75 =$

5) $0.95 \times 0.7 =$

6) $1.57 \times 0.9 =$

7) $5.85 \times 1.3 =$

8) $12.5 \times 4.5 =$

9) $19.8 \times 7.32 =$

10) $85.1 \times 1.5 =$

11) $79.5 \times 11.2 =$

12) $86.9 \times 21.5 =$

✎ **Find the quotient.**

13) $3.25 \div 10 =$

14) $24.5 \div 100 =$

15) $3.9 \div 3 =$

16) $91.2 \div 0.6 =$

17) $29.2 \div 0.4 =$

18) $38.7 \div \,`9 =$

19) $297.8 \div 1,000 =$

20) $53.55 \div 0.7 =$

21) $345.45 \div 0.1 =$

22) $70.27 \div 0.25 =$

23) $28.968 \div 0.3 =$

24) $86.34 \div 0.06 =$

Comparing Decimals

✎ **Write the correct comparison symbol (>, < or =).**

1) 0.80 ☐ 0.080

2) 0.086 ☐ 0.86

3) 7.090 ☐ 7.09

4) 3.25 ☐ 3.06

5) 4.09 ☐ 0.490

6) 6.06 ☐ 6.6

7) 6.08 ☐ 6.080

8) 4.05 ☐ 4.2

9) 12.35 ☐ 12.198

10) 0.957 ☐ 0.0957

11) 25.24 ☐ 25.240

12) 0.742 ☐ 0.752

13) 14.09 ☐ 14.10

14) 17.45 ☐ 17.154

15) 11.44 ☐ 11.439

16) 15.41 ☐ 15.410

17) 21.43 ☐ 21.043

18) 8.098 ☐ 8.90

19) 16.044 ☐ 16.040

20) 32.35 ☐ 32.350

Rounding Decimals

✍ Round each decimal to the nearest whole number.

1) 56.27	3) 18.32	5) 7.90
2) 5.9	4) 4.8	6) 57.7

✍ Round each decimal to the nearest tenth.

7) 42.785	9) 96.586	11) 27.198
8) 15.224	10) 101.78	12) 96.87

✍ Round each decimal to the nearest hundredth.

13) 9.648	15) 89.2882	17) 68.229
14) 27.819	16) 120.912	18) 85.642

✍ Round each decimal to the nearest thousandth.

19) 19.88486	21) 145.9322	23) 189.0991
20) 46.72611	22) 210.1581	24) 121.76798

Answers of Worksheets – Chapter 2

Simplifying Fractions

1) $\frac{1}{2}$

2) $\frac{4}{5}$

3) $\frac{3}{4}$

4) $\frac{1}{2}$

5) $\frac{1}{4}$

6) $\frac{2}{3}$

7) $\frac{4}{5}$

8) $\frac{1}{4}$

9) $\frac{1}{2}$

10) $\frac{5}{7}$

11) $\frac{1}{4}$

12) $\frac{1}{2}$

13) $\frac{7}{8}$

14) $\frac{9}{10}$

15) $\frac{1}{3}$

16) $\frac{5}{14}$

17) $\frac{2}{5}$

18) $\frac{4}{27}$

19) $\frac{6}{31}$

20) $\frac{4}{9}$

21) $\frac{1}{8}$

22) C

23) A

24) B

Adding and Subtracting Fractions

1) $\frac{8x}{8} = x$

2) $\frac{9x}{14}$

3) $\frac{7x}{12}$

4) $\frac{31x}{40}$

5) $\frac{17xy}{35}$

6) $\frac{2x}{3}$

7) $\frac{11a}{12}$

8) $\frac{6}{x}$

9) $\frac{a+2b}{ab}$

10) $\frac{31b}{35}$

11) $\frac{4a}{y}$

12) $\frac{7}{2x}$

13) $\frac{x}{6}$

14) $\frac{x}{40}$

15) $\frac{x-y}{7}$

16) $\frac{5x}{42}$

17) $\frac{7a}{45}$

18) $\frac{ab}{2}$

19) $\frac{2}{3x}$

20) $\frac{13}{4y}$

21) $\frac{3}{x}$

22) $\frac{19}{3ab}$

23) $\frac{5a}{3y}$

24) $\frac{13}{3b}$

25) $\frac{a}{b}$

26) $\frac{3b-2a}{ab}$

27) $\frac{10a}{3b}$

28) $\frac{5}{2xy}$

29) $\frac{7}{4a}$

30) $\frac{2a}{9b}$

Multiplying and Dividing Fractions

1) $\frac{5}{a}$

2) $\frac{3}{b}$

3) $\frac{1}{6}$

4) $\frac{1}{2}$

5) $\frac{x}{2y}$

6) $\frac{1}{2}$

7) $\frac{1}{a}$

8) $\frac{8a}{5}$

9) $\frac{2}{3}$

10) $\frac{6}{b}$

11) $\frac{b}{3}$

12) $\frac{2b}{d}$

13) 2

14) 3

15) $\frac{a}{3}$

16) $\frac{1}{6}$

17) $\frac{3}{b}$

18) $\frac{8}{3}$

19) $\frac{2}{3}$

20) $\frac{3a}{8}$

21) $\frac{3}{8}$

22) 1

23) $\frac{1}{10}$

24) $\frac{7}{8}$

25) $\frac{5}{3y}$

26) $\frac{4}{3}$

27) b

28) $\frac{4}{b}$

29) $\frac{3b}{2}$

30) $\frac{2}{x}$

Adding and Subtracting Mixed Numbers

1) $6\frac{1}{6}$

2) $5\frac{3}{5}$

3) $11\frac{7}{8}$

4) $6\frac{1}{6}$

5) $6\frac{14}{15}$

6) $11\frac{7}{16}$

7) $8\frac{23}{30}$

8) $11\frac{7}{12}$

9) $11\frac{5}{42}$

10) $14\frac{19}{48}$

11) $1\frac{1}{2}$

12) 2

13) $3\frac{2}{9}$

14) $4\frac{1}{12}$

15) $4\frac{1}{18}$

16) $3\frac{1}{8}$

17) $3\frac{3}{10}$

18) $3\frac{13}{30}$

19) $5\frac{11}{35}$

20) $3\frac{15}{16}$

21) $1\frac{1}{5}$

22) $1\frac{7}{10}$

23) $7\frac{4}{5}$

24) $2\frac{13}{36}$

25) $9\frac{5}{18}$

26) $8\frac{25}{42}$

Multiplying and Dividing Mixed Numbers

1) $10\frac{1}{2}$

2) $9\frac{4}{5}$

3) $27\frac{3}{5}$

4) $29\frac{1}{56}$

5) $23\frac{8}{33}$

6) $40\frac{11}{72}$

7) $144\frac{7}{18}$

8) $64\frac{1}{45}$

9) $49\frac{7}{36}$

10) 27

11) $1\frac{6}{11}$

12) $1\frac{11}{14}$

13) $1\frac{43}{45}$

14) $3\frac{1}{12}$

15) $1\frac{27}{50}$

16) $1\frac{4}{93}$

17) $2\frac{29}{51}$

18) $1\frac{1}{113}$

19) $3\frac{1}{68}$

20) $2\frac{44}{47}$

21) $1\frac{35}{39}$

22) $\frac{326}{327}$ 24) $1\frac{19}{66}$ 26) $2\frac{1}{60}$

23) $1\frac{107}{108}$ 25) $2\frac{109}{138}$

Adding and Subtracting Decimals

1) 30.91	6) 61.7	11) 1.28	16) 2.43
2) 74.58	7) 52.57	12) 3.75	17) 37.79
3) 84.35	8) 106.66	13) 2.1	18) 2.28
4) 30.35	9) 79.07	14) 5.3	19) 24.7
5) 72.94	10) 1.6	15) 28.15	

Multiplying and Dividing Decimals

1) 0.48	7) 7.605	13) 0.325	19) 0.2978
2) 2.25	8) 56.25	14) 0.245	20) 76.5
3) 0.348	9) 144.936	15) 1.3	21) 3,454.5
4) 0.1125	10) 127.65	16) 152	22) 281.08
5) 0.665	11) 890.4	17) 73	23) 96.56
6) 1.413	12) 1,868.35	18) 4.3	24) 1,439

Comparing Decimals

1) >	6) <	11) =	16) =
2) <	7) =	12) <	17) >
3) =	8) <	13) <	18) <
4) >	9) >	14) >	19) >
5) >	10) >	15) >	20) =

Rounding Decimals

1) 56	9) 96.6	17) 68.23
2) 6	10) 101.8	18) 85.64
3) 18	11) 27.2	19) 19.885
4) 5	12) 96.9	20) 46.726
5) 8	13) 9.65	21) 145.932
6) 58	14) 27.82	22) 210.158
7) 42.8	15) 89.29	23) 189.099
8) 15.2	16) 120.91	24) 121.768

Chapter 3:
Proportions, Ratios, and Percent

Topics that you will practice in this chapter:

- ✓ Simplifying Ratios
- ✓ Proportional Ratios
- ✓ Similarity and Ratios
- ✓ Ratio and Rates Word Problems
- ✓ Percentage Calculations
- ✓ Percent Problems
- ✓ Discount, Tax and Tip
- ✓ Percent of Change
- ✓ Simple Interest

Without mathematics, there's nothing you can do. Everything around you is mathematics. Everything around you is numbers." – Shakuntala Devi

Simplifying Ratios

✎ **Reduce each ratio.**

1) $15:20 =$ ___: ___

2) $9:90 =$ ___: ___

3) $24:42 =$ ___: ___

4) $7:21 =$ ___: ___

5) $11:110$ ___: ___

6) $8:64 =$ ___: ___

7) $18:72 =$ ___: ___

8) $10:25 =$ ___: ___

9) $7:42 =$ ___: ___

10) $49:63 =$ ___: ___

11) $12:18$ ___: ___

12) $35:10$ ___: ___

13) $150:15$ ___: ___

14) $2.4:3.2$ ___: ___

15) $7:56 =$ ___: ___

16) $45:63$ ___: ___

17) $77:99$ ___: ___

18) $39:13$ ___: ___

19) $15:45$ ___: ___

20) $84:12$ ___: ___

21) $25:5$ ___: ___

22) $70:56$ ___: ___

23) $70:140$ ___: ___

24) $1.2:36$ ___: ___

✎ **Write each ratio as a fraction in simplest form.**

25) $7:14 =$

26) $27:45 =$

27) $24:56 =$

28) $16:48 =$

29) $22:66 =$

30) $21:98 =$

31) $34:68 =$

32) $6:30 =$

33) $35:84 =$

34) $12:54 =$

35) $88:104 =$

36) $36:81 =$

37) $1.5:18 =$

38) $4.5:16.5 =$

39) $5:75 =$

40) $3.1:12.4 =$

41) $1.6:6.4 =$

42) $0.25:1.25 =$

43) $8.8:16.4 =$

44) $0.75:6.75 =$

45) $1.8:3 =$

Proportional Ratios

✍ **Fill in the blanks; Calculate each proportion.**

1) $3 : 8 = \_\_ : 32$

2) $1 : 2 = 45 : \_\_$

3) $1 : 11 = \_\_ : 55$

4) $9 : 12 = 18 : \_\_$

5) $9 : 7 = 81 : \_\_$

6) $2 : 8 = \_\_ : 56$

7) $2.3 : 1.2 = \_\_ : 12$

8) $0.5 : 2 = \_\_ : 32$

9) $1.6 : 2 = \_\_ : 60$

10) $2.5 : 4.5 = \_\_ : 90$

11) $3.8 : 7.1 = 7.6 : \_\_$

12) $5.5 : 6 = 16.5 : \_\_$

✍ **State if each pair of ratios form a proportion.**

13) $\frac{5}{12}$ and $\frac{15}{36}$

14) $\frac{2}{4}$ and $\frac{18}{36}$

15) $\frac{7}{8}$ and $\frac{28}{32}$

16) $\frac{3}{8}$ and $\frac{27}{64}$

17) $\frac{1}{14}$ and $\frac{5}{65}$

18) $\frac{7}{11}$ and $\frac{70}{100}$

19) $\frac{12}{15}$ and $\frac{48}{60}$

20) $\frac{3}{17}$ and $\frac{36}{204}$

21) $\frac{1.2}{1.5}$ and $\frac{1.44}{22.5}$

22) $\frac{1.3}{1.1}$ and $\frac{3.9}{33}$

23) $\frac{0.7}{0.9}$ and $\frac{6.3}{8.1}$

24) $\frac{2.4}{3.2}$ and $\frac{48}{64}$

✍ **Calculate each proportion.**

25) $\frac{14}{16} = \frac{21}{x}$, $x = \_\_\_\_$

26) $\frac{3}{28} = \frac{42}{x}$, $x = \_\_\_\_$

27) $\frac{19}{5} = \frac{38}{x}$, $x = \_\_\_\_$

28) $\frac{3}{10} = \frac{x}{140}$, $x = \_\_\_$

29) $\frac{4}{9} = \frac{x}{108}$, $x = \_\_\_\_$

30) $\frac{7}{32} = \frac{21}{x}$, $x = \_\_\_$

31) $\frac{9}{8} = \frac{108}{x}$, $x = \_\_\_$

32) $\frac{12}{17} = \frac{48}{x}$, $x = \_\_\_$

33) $\frac{1.4}{5} = \frac{x}{30}$, $x = \_\_\_\_$

34) $\frac{1.6}{12} = \frac{x}{60}$, $x = \_\_\_$

35) $\frac{3.5}{15} = \frac{x}{315}$, $x = \_\_\_$

36) $\frac{4.7}{2.5} = \frac{x}{50}$, $x = \_\_\_$

Similarity and Ratios

✎ **Each pair of figures is similar. Find the missing side.**

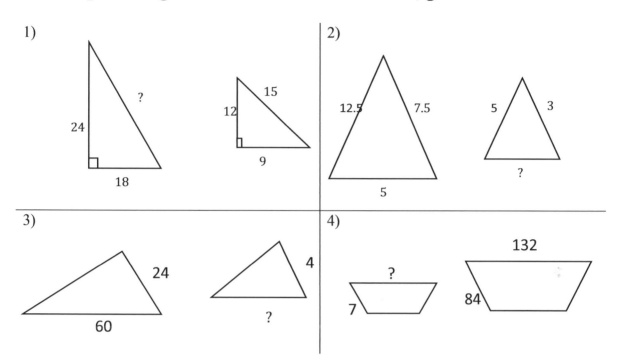

1)

2)

3)

4)

✎ **Calculate.**

5) Two rectangles are similar. The first is 14 feet wide and 70 feet long. The second is 30 feet wide. What is the length of the second rectangle? _____

6) Two rectangles are similar. One is 3.2 meters by 15 meters. The longer side of the second rectangle is 42 meters. What is the other side of the second rectangle? _____

7) A building casts a shadow 24 ft long. At the same time a girl 10 ft tall casts a shadow 6 ft long. How tall is the building? _____

8) The scale of a map of Texas is 8 inches: 52 miles. If you measure the distance from Dallas to Martin County as 28.8 inches, approximately how far is Martin County from Dallas? _____

Ratio and Rates Word Problems

✎ **Find the answer for each word problem.**

1) Mason has 32 red cards and 40 green cards. What is the ratio of Mason 's red cards to his green cards? _____

2) In a party, 24 soft drinks are required for every 42 guests. If there are 378 guests, how many soft drinks is required? _____

3) In Mason's class, 54 of the students are tall and 30 are short. In Michael's class 126 students are tall and 70 students are short. Which class has a higher ratio of tall to short students? _____

4) The price of 4 apples at the Quick Market is $3.65. The price of 6 of the same apples at Walmart is $4.25. Which place is the better buy? _____

5) The bakers at a Bakery can make 90 bagels in 3 hours. How many bagels can they bake in 17 hours? What is that rate per hour? _____

6) You can buy 8 cans of green beans at a supermarket for $5.60. How much does it cost to buy 56 cans of green beans? _____

7) The ratio of boys to girls in a class is 4: 7. If there are 16 boys in the class, how many girls are in that class? _____

8) The ratio of red marbles to blue marbles in a bag is 3: 4. If there are 42 marbles in the bag, how many of the marbles are red? _____

Percentage Calculations

✎ **Calculate the given percent of each value.**

1) 3% *of* 60 = ____

2) 20% *of* 80 = ____

3) 25% *of* 80 = ____

4) 24% *of* 50 = ____

5) 18% *of* 150 = ____

6) 70% *of* 35 = ____

7) 15% *of* 28 = ____

8) 32% *of* 300 = ____

9) 54% *of* 80 = ____

10) 10% *of* 610 = ____

11) 35% *of* 520 = ____

12) 64% *of* 110 = ____

13) 44% *of* 200 = ____

14) 28% *of* 94 = ____

15) 30% *of* 85 = ____

16) 68% *of* 102 = ____

17) 45% *of* 160 = ____

18) 55% *of* 220 = ____

✎ **Calculate the percent of each given value.**

19) ____% *of* 18 = 9

20) ____% *of* 50 = 40

21) ____% *of* 140 = 7

22) ____% *of* 158 = 39.5

23) ____% *of* 75 = 9.375

24) ____% *of* 45 = 11.25

25) ____% *of* 90 = 22.5

26) ____% *of* 650 = 19.5

27) ____% *of* 480 = 24

28) ___% *of* 400 = 57.32

✎ **Calculate each percent problem.**

29) A Cinema has 132 seats. 92 seats were sold for the current movie. What percent of seats are empty? _____ %

30) There are 52 boys and 68 girls in a class. 55.00% of the students in the class take the bus to school. How many students do not take the bus to school? ____

Percent Problems

✍ Calculate each problem.

1) 30 is what percent of 60? ____%

2) 32 is what percent of 80? ____%

3) 72 is what percent of 45? ____%

4) 8 is what percent of 200? ____%

5) 9 is what percent of 600? ____%

6) 30 is what percent of 500? ____%

7) 70 is what percent of 350? ____%

8) 44 is what percent of 550? ____%

9) 270 is what percent of 900? ____%

10) 180 is what percent of 720? ___%

11) 37.5 is what percent of 75? ___%

12) 27.5 is what percent of 55? ___%

13) 60 is what percent of 750? ___%

14) 22.5 is what percent of 18? ___%

15) 36 is what percent of 24? ___%

16) 18 is what percent of 60? ___%

17) 140 is what percent of 280? ___%

18) 128 is what percent of 40? ___%

✍ Calculate each percent word problem.

19) There are 32 employees in a company. On a certain day, 24 were present. What percent showed up for work? _____%

20) A metal bar weighs 36 ounces. 40% of the bar is gold. How many ounces of gold are in the bar? _____

21) A crew is made up of 12 women; the rest are men. If 20% of the crew are women, how many people are in the crew? _____

22) There are 32 students in a class and 8 of them are girls. What percent are boys? _____%

23) The Royals softball team played 310 games and won 248 of them. What percent of the games did they lose? _____%

Discount, Tax and Tip

✍ Find the selling price of each item.

1) Original price of a computer: $450

Tax: 8% Selling price: $_____

2) Original price of a laptop: $240

Tax: 4% Selling price: $_____

3) Original price of a sofa: $900

Tax: 12%   Selling price: $_____

4) Original price of a car: $10,400

Tax: 2.5%   Selling price: $_____

5) Original price of a Table: $400

Tax: 3% Selling price: $_____

6) Original price of a house: $360,000

Tax: 2.8%   Selling price: $_____

7) Original price of a tablet: $150

Discount: 24%   Selling price: $____

8) Original price of a chair: $180

Discount: 20%   Selling price: $____

9) Original price of a book: $80

Discount: 30%   Selling price: $____

10) Original price of a cellphone: $800

Discount: 20%   Selling price: $___

11) Food bill: $56

Tip:15%   Price: $_____

12) Food bill: $50

Tipp: 10%   Price: $_____

13) Food bill: $94

Tip: 25%   Price: $_____

14) Food bill: $48

Tipp: 30%   Price: $_____

✍ Find the answer for each word problem.

15) Nicolas hired a moving company. The company charged $400 for its services, and Nicolas gives the movers a 20% tip. How much does Nicolas tip the movers? $_____

16) Mason has lunch at a restaurant and the cost of his meal is $80. Mason wants to leave a 20% tip. What is Mason's total bill including tip? $_____

17) The sales tax in Texas is 14.45% and an item costs $300. How much is the tax? $_____

18) The price of a table at Best Buy is $520. If the sales tax is 4%, what is the final price of the table including tax? $_____

Percent of Change

✍ **Find each percent of change.**

1) From 300 to 600. ___ %

2) From 45 ft to 225 ft. ___ %

3) From $60 to $420. ___ %

4) From 30 cm to 120 cm. ___ %

5) From 10 to 30. ___ %

6) From 12 to 30. ___ %

7) From 140 to 210. ___ %

8) From 800 to 400. ___ %

9) From 85 to 51. ___ %

10) From 152 to 76. ___ %

✍ **Calculate each percent of change word problem.**

11) Bob got a raise, and his hourly wage increased from $32 to $40. What is the percent increase? ___ %

12) The price of a pair of shoes increases from $70 to $112. What is the percent increase? ___ %

13) At a coffee shop, the price of a cup of coffee increased from $1.90 to $2.28. What is the percent increase in the cost of the coffee? ___ %

14) 30 cm are cut from a 120 cm board. What is the percent decrease in length? ___ %

15) In a class, the number of students has been increased from 54 to 81. What is the percent increase? ___ %

16) The price of gasoline rose from $22.4 to $25.76 in one month. By what percent did the gas price rise? ___ %

17) A shirt was originally priced at $19. It went on sale for $22.80. What was the percent that the shirt was discounted? ___ %

Simple Interest

✎ Determine the simple interest for these loans.

1) $210 at 15% for 4 years. $ _____

6) $28,000 at 3.5% for 6 years. $ _____

2) $1,200 at 6% for 3 years. $ _____

7) $9,600 at 8% for 2 years. $ _____

3) $950 at 25% for 2 years. $ _____

8) $500 at 4.2% for 5 years. $ _____

4) $6,500 at 1.5% for 7 months. $ ____

9) $700 at 2.8 % for 6 months. $ _____

5) $240 at 5% for 8 months. $ _____

10) $9,000 at 1.6% for 4 years. $ _____

✎ Calculate each simple interest word problem.

11) A new car, valued at $16,000, depreciates at 3.5% per year. What is the value of the car two year after purchase? $_____

12) Sara puts $9,000 into an investment yielding 8% annual simple interest; she left the money in for three years. How much interest does Sara get at the end of those three years? $_____

13) A bank is offering 12.5% simple interest on a savings account. If you deposit $32,400, how much interest will you earn in one years? $_____

14) $2,400 interest is earned on a principal of $10,000 at a simple interest rate of 12% interest per year. For how many years was the principal invested? _____

15) In how many years will $1,200 yield an interest of $384 at 8% simple interest?

_____

16) Jim invested $5,000 in a bond at a yearly rate of 2.5%. He earned $375 in interest. How long was the money invested? _____

Answers of Worksheets – Chapter 3

Simplifying Ratios

1) 3:4
2) 1:10
3) 4:7
4) 1:3
5) 1:10
6) 1:8
7) 2:8
8) 2:5
9) 1:6
10) 7:9
11) 2:3
12) 7:2
13) 10:1

14) 3:4
15) 1:8
16) 5:7
17) 7:9
18) 3:1
19) 1:3
20) 7:1
21) 5:1
22) 5:4
23) 1:2
24) 1:30
25) $\frac{1}{2}$

26) $\frac{3}{5}$
27) $\frac{3}{7}$
28) $\frac{1}{3}$
29) $\frac{1}{3}$
30) $\frac{3}{14}$
31) $\frac{1}{2}$
32) $\frac{1}{5}$
33) $\frac{5}{12}$
34) $\frac{2}{9}$
35) $\frac{11}{13}$

36) $\frac{4}{9}$
37) $\frac{1}{12}$
38) $\frac{3}{11}$
39) $\frac{1}{15}$
40) $\frac{1}{4}$
41) $\frac{4}{3}$
42) $\frac{1}{5}$
43) $\frac{22}{41}$
44) $\frac{1}{9}$
45) $\frac{3}{5}$

Proportional Ratios

1) 12
2) 90
3) 5
4) 24
5) 63
6) 14
7) 23
8) 8
9) 48

10) 50
11) 14.2
12) 18
13) Yes
14) Yes
15) Yes
16) No
17) No
18) No

19) Yes
20) Yes
21) No
22) No
23) Yes
24) Yes
25) 24
26) 392
27) 10

28) 42
29) 48
30) 96
31) 96
32) 68
33) 8.4
34) 8
35) 73.5
36) 94

Similarity and ratios

1) 30
2) 2
3) 10

4) 11
5) 150 feet
6) 8.96 meters

7) 40 feet
8) 187.2 miles

Ratio and Rates Word Problems

1) 4:5

2) 252

3) The ratio for both classes is 9 to 5. 6) $39.20

4) Walmart is a better buy. 7) 28

5) 510, the rate is 30 per hour. 8) 18

Percentage Calculations

1) 1.8	11) 182	21) 5%
2) 1.6	12) 70.4	22) 25%
3) 20	13) 88	23) 12.5%
4) 12	14) 26.32	24) 25%
5) 27	15) 25.5	25) 25%
6) 24.5	16) 69.36	26) 3%
7) 4.2	17) 72	27) 5%
8) 96	18) 121	28) 14.33%
9) 43.2	19) 50%	29) 30.30%
10) 61	20) 80%	30) 54

Percent Problems

1) 50%	9) 30%	17) 50%
2) 40%	10) 25%	18) 320%
3) 160%	11) 50%	19) 75%
4) 4%	12) 50%	20) 14.4 ounces
5) 1.5%	13) 8%	21) 60
6) 6%	14) 125%	22) 75%
7) 20%	15) 150%	23) 20%
8) 8%	16) 30%	

Discount, Tax and Tip

1) $486.00	7) $144.00	13) $117.50
2) $249.60	8) $144.00	14) $62.40
3) $1,008.00	9) $56.00	15) $80.00
4) $10,660.00	10) $640.00	16) $96.00
5) $412.00	11) $64.40	17) $43.35
6) $370,080	12) $55.00	18) $540.80

Percent of Change

1) 100%	7) 50%	13) 20%
2) 400%	8) 50%	14) 25%
3) 600%	9) 40%	15) 50%
4) 300%	10) 50%	16) 15%
5) 200%	11) 25%	17) 20%
6) 150%	12) 60%	

Simple Interest

1) $126.00	7) $1,536.00	13) $4,050.00
2) $216.00	8) $105.00	14) 2 years
3) $475.00	9) $9.80	15) 4 years
4) $56.875	10) $576.00	16) 3 years
5) $8.00	11) $14,880.00	
6) $5,880.00	12) $2,160.00	

Chapter 4:

Exponents and Radicals Expressions

Topics that you will practice in this chapter:

- ✓ Multiplication Property of Exponents
- ✓ Zero and Negative Exponents
- ✓ Division Property of Exponents
- ✓ Powers of Products and Quotients
- ✓ Negative Exponents and Negative Bases
- ✓ Scientific Notation
- ✓ Square Roots
- ✓ Simplifying Radical Expressions
- ✓ Simplifying Radical Expressions Involving Fractions
- ✓ Multiplying Radical Expressions
- ✓ Adding and Subtracting Radical Expressions
- ✓ Domain and Range of Radical Functions
- ✓ Solving Radical Equations

Mathematics is no more computation than typing is literature.
– John Allen Paulos

Multiplication Property of Exponents

✎ Simplify and write the answer in exponential form.

1) $2 \times 2^5 =$

2) $7^2 \times 7 =$

3) $8^3 \times 8^3 =$

4) $9^4 \times 9^3 =$

5) $4^2 \times 4^4 \times 4 =$

6) $5 \times 5^2 \times 5^3 =$

7) $9^3 \times 9^3 \times 9 \times 9 =$

8) $4x \times x =$

9) $x^5 \times x^3 =$

10) $x^6 \times x^2 =$

11) $x^2 \times x^4 \times x^5 =$

12) $7x \times 7x =$

13) $4x^2 \times 5x^3 =$

14) $12x^3 \times x =$

15) $3x^2 \times 3x^2 \times 3x^2 =$

16) $7x^5 \times 2x^3 =$

17) $x^8 \times 2x =$

18) $3x \times 3x^3 =$

19) $6x^2 \times 2x^5 =$

20) $3yx^3 \times 12x =$

21) $8x^3 \times y^5x^2 =$

22) $4y^7x^2 \times 3y^2x^5 =$

23) $9yx^2 \times 4x^5y^2 =$

24) $10x^4 \times 11x^4y^4 =$

25) $9x^3y^4 \times 9x^6y^2 =$

26) $12x^4y^4 \times 6xy^3 =$

27) $9xy^4 \times 11x^3y^3 =$

28) $6x^2y^4 \times 8x^3y^6 =$

29) $8x \times y^7x^2 \times 5y^3 =$

30) $3yx^3 \times 2y^3x^2 \times 7xy =$

31) $8yx^5 \times 3y^4x \times 3xy^3 =$

32) $9x^3 \times 11y^4x^3 \times 2yx^4 =$

Zero and Negative Exponents

✎ **Evaluate the following expressions.**

1) $1^{-5} =$

2) $2^{-4} =$

3) $2^{-5} =$

4) $3^0 =$

5) $3^{-2} =$

6) $2^{-7} =$

7) $13^{-2} =$

8) $14^{-2} =$

9) $2^{-8} =$

10) $20^{-2} =$

11) $19^{-1} =$

12) $3^{-6} =$

13) $15^{-2} =$

14) $10^{-2} =$

15) $16^{-2} =$

16) $30^{-2} =$

17) $8^{-4} =$

18) $3^{-7} =$

19) $2^{-10} =$

20) $10^{-3} =$

21) $18^{-2} =$

22) $25^{-2} =$

23) $40^{-2} =$

24) $50^{-2} =$

25) $11^{-3} =$

26) $22^{-2} =$

27) $17^{-2} =$

28) $3^{-8} =$

29) $4^{-5} =$

30) $60^{-2} =$

31) $\left(\frac{1}{3}\right)^{-2} =$

32) $\left(\frac{1}{5}\right)^{-3} =$

33) $\left(\frac{1}{8}\right)^{-2} =$

34) $\left(\frac{2}{5}\right)^{-2} =$

35) $\left(\frac{1}{15}\right)^{-2} =$

36) $\left(\frac{7}{12}\right)^{-2} =$

37) $\left(\frac{1}{20}\right)^{-2} =$

38) $\left(\frac{1}{7}\right)^{-3} =$

39) $\left(\frac{2}{3}\right)^{-5} =$

40) $\left(\frac{9}{11}\right)^{-1} =$

41) $\left(\frac{8}{9}\right)^{-2} =$

42) $\left(\frac{1}{8}\right)^{-3} =$

Division Property of Exponents

✎ **Simplify.**

1) $\dfrac{5^2}{5^6} =$

2) $\dfrac{6^9}{6^5} =$

3) $\dfrac{9^7}{9} =$

4) $\dfrac{3}{3^3} =$

5) $\dfrac{2x}{x^8} =$

6) $\dfrac{4 \times 4^5}{4^5 \times 4^2} =$

7) $\dfrac{12^6}{12^2} =$

8) $\dfrac{7 \times 7^9}{7^2 \times 7^4} =$

9) $\dfrac{4^5 \times 4^8}{4^2 \times 4^{11}} =$

10) $\dfrac{20x}{40x^4} =$

11) $\dfrac{8x^9}{9x^6} =$

12) $\dfrac{24x^3}{16x^5} =$

13) $\dfrac{25x^2}{50y^8} =$

14) $\dfrac{60xy^5}{12x^4y^2} =$

15) $\dfrac{8x^7}{12x} =$

16) $\dfrac{48x^2y^4}{16x^5} =$

17) $\dfrac{50x^6}{25x^9y^{14}} =$

18) $\dfrac{90yx^8}{15yx^9} =$

19) $\dfrac{18x^9y}{36x^{12}y^3} =$

20) $\dfrac{9x^8}{81x^8} =$

21) $\dfrac{9x^{-7}}{11x^{-3}} =$

Powers of Products and Quotients

✎ **Simplify.**

1) $(4^2)^3 =$

2) $(5^2)^2 =$

3) $(3 \times 3^2)^3 =$

4) $(3 \times 2^3)^2 =$

5) $(15^2 \times 15^2)^5 =$

6) $(7^2 \times 7^3)^4 =$

7) $(9 \times 9^2)^2 =$

8) $(4^6)^3 =$

9) $(7x^7)^3 =$

10) $(8x^4y^3)^2 =$

11) $(3x^3y^2)^4 =$

12) $(4x^2y^2)^2 =$

13) $(3x^5y^2)^3 =$

14) $(4x^3y^2)^3 =$

15) $(2x^3x)^5 =$

16) $(6x^4x^2)^2 =$

17) $(7x^{12}y^5)^2 =$

18) $(5x^7x^4)^3 =$

19) $(8x^2 \times 6x)^2 =$

20) $(9x^{14}y^3)^3 =$

21) $(5x^4y^2)^4 =$

22) $(3x^3y^7)^5 =$

23) $(8x \times 2y^3)^2 =$

24) $\left(\dfrac{8x}{x^3}\right)^3 =$

25) $\left(\dfrac{x^4y^5}{x^3y^5}\right)^7 =$

26) $\left(\dfrac{36xy}{6x^5}\right)^2 =$

27) $\left(\dfrac{x^4}{x^5y^2}\right)^3 =$

28) $\left(\dfrac{xy^2}{x^3y^8}\right)^{-3} =$

29) $\left(\dfrac{5xy^7}{x^2}\right)^3 =$

30) $\left(\dfrac{xy^5}{2xy^3}\right)^{-6} =$

Negative Exponents and Negative Bases

✒ **Simplify.**

1) $-4^{-2} =$

2) $-7^{-1} =$

3) $-5^{-2} =$

4) $-x^{-9} =$

5) $10x^{-2} =$

6) $-7x^{-4} =$

7) $-15x^{-4} =$

8) $-15x^{-7}y^{-4} =$

9) $32x^{-9}y^{-3} =$

10) $45a^{-7}b^{-3} =$

11) $-25x^3y^{-5} =$

12) $-\dfrac{18}{x^{-9}} =$

13) $-\dfrac{13x}{a^{-8}} =$

14) $\left(-\dfrac{1}{3}\right)^{-4} =$

15) $\left(-\dfrac{3}{4}\right)^{-3} =$

16) $-\dfrac{12}{a^{-6}b^{-4}} =$

17) $-\dfrac{48x}{x^{-6}} =$

18) $-\dfrac{a^{-12}}{b^{-5}} =$

19) $-\dfrac{27}{x^{-5}} =$

20) $\dfrac{12b}{-48c^{-6}} =$

21) $\dfrac{24ab}{a^{-4}b^{-3}} =$

22) $-\dfrac{8n^{-7}}{40p^{-9}} =$

23) $\dfrac{9ab^{-6}}{-5c^{-2}} =$

24) $\left(\dfrac{2a}{3c}\right)^{-4} =$

25) $\left(-\dfrac{8x}{5yz}\right)^{-2} =$

26) $\dfrac{9ab^{-6}}{-4c^{-3}} =$

27) $\left(-\dfrac{x^3}{x^4}\right)^{-5} =$

28) $\left(-\dfrac{x^{-3}}{3x^3}\right)^{-3} =$

29) $\left(-\dfrac{x^{-6}}{x^4}\right)^{-3} =$

Scientific Notation

✎ **Write each number in scientific notation.**

1) $0.226 =$

2) $0.05 =$

3) $4.8 =$

4) $90 =$

5) $120 =$

6) $0.123 =$

7) $82 =$

8) $5,400 =$

9) $2,460 =$

10) $75,300 =$

11) $61,000,000 =$

12) $0.00009 =$

13) $468,000 =$

14) $0.00458 =$

15) $0.000087 =$

16) $31,800,000 =$

17) $950,000 =$

18) $9,000,000,000 =$

19) $0.0007 =$

20) $0.00041 =$

✎ **Write each number in standard notation.**

21) $4 \times 10^{-2} =$

22) $7 \times 10^{-4} =$

23) $4.3 \times 10^{6} =$

24) $7 \times 10^{-4} =$

25) $8.7 \times 10^{-3} =$

26) $12 \times 10^{5} =$

27) $35 \times 10^{3} =$

28) $1.89 \times 10^{5} =$

29) $13 \times 10^{-6} =$

30) $7.3 \times 10^{-4} =$

Square Roots

✎ **Find the value each square root.**

1) $\sqrt{64} = $ ___

2) $\sqrt{4} = $ ___

3) $\sqrt{289} = $ ___

4) $\sqrt{0.25} = $ ___

5) $\sqrt{0.01} = $ ___

6) $\sqrt{0.09} = $ ___

7) $\sqrt{1,600} = $ ___

8) $\sqrt{2.25} = $ ___

9) $\sqrt{0} = $ ___

10) $\sqrt{0.04} = $ ___

11) $\sqrt{0.36} = $ ___

12) $\sqrt{0.81} = $ ___

13) $\sqrt{0.49} = $ ___

14) $\sqrt{1.21} = $ ___

15) $\sqrt{1.69} = $ ___

16) $\sqrt{0.16} = $ ___

17) $\sqrt{529} = $ ___

18) $\sqrt{625} = $ ___

19) $\sqrt{0.81} = $ ___

20) $\sqrt{20} = $ ___

21) $\sqrt{50} = $ ___

22) $\sqrt{676} = $ ___

23) $\sqrt{270} = $ ___

24) $\sqrt{32} = $ ___

✎ **Evaluate.**

25) $\sqrt{4} \times \sqrt{16} = $ _____

26) $\sqrt{49} \times \sqrt{64} = $ _____

27) $\sqrt{2} \times \sqrt{8} = $ _____

28) $\sqrt{17} \times \sqrt{17} = $ _____

29) $\sqrt{13} \times \sqrt{13} = $ _____

30) $\sqrt{15} \times \sqrt{15} = $ _____

31) $\sqrt{19} + \sqrt{19} = $ _____

32) $\sqrt{1} + \sqrt{1} = $ _____

33) $8\sqrt{7} - 2\sqrt{7} = $ _____

34) $7\sqrt{10} \times 6\sqrt{10} = $ _____

35) $9\sqrt{5} \times 2\sqrt{5} = $ _____

36) $8\sqrt{3} - \sqrt{12} = $ _____

Simplifying Radical Expressions

✎ **Simplify.**

1) $\sqrt{13y^2} =$

2) $\sqrt{60x^3} =$

3) $\sqrt[3]{27a} =$

4) $\sqrt{81x^2} =$

5) $\sqrt{150a} =$

6) $\sqrt[3]{135w^3} =$

7) $\sqrt{200x} =$

8) $\sqrt{192v} =$

9) $\sqrt[3]{64x} =$

10) $\sqrt{84x^3} =$

11) $\sqrt{121x^2} =$

12) $\sqrt[3]{48a} =$

13) $\sqrt{480} =$

14) $\sqrt{1,575p^2} =$

15) $\sqrt{108m^6} =$

16) $\sqrt{198x^3y^2} =$

17) $\sqrt{169x^2y^3} =$

18) $\sqrt{25a^6} =$

19) $\sqrt{50x^2y^3} =$

20) $\sqrt[3]{512y^3} =$

21) $2\sqrt{144x^2} =$

22) $3\sqrt{400x^2} =$

23) $\sqrt[3]{189xy^4} =$

24) $\sqrt[3]{1,331x^3y^5} =$

25) $3\sqrt{150a} =$

26) $\sqrt[3]{729y} =$

27) $3\sqrt{18xyr^3} =$

28) $6\sqrt{225x^2yz^6} =$

29) $3\sqrt[3]{125x^3y^2} =$

30) $7\sqrt{12a^2bc^4} =$

31) $4\sqrt[3]{1,000x^9y^{15}} =$

Answers of Worksheets – Chapter 4

Multiplication Property of Exponents

1) 2^6

2) 7^3

3) 8^6

4) 9^7

5) 4^7

6) 5^6

7) 9^8

8) $4x^2$

9) x^8

10) x^8

11) x^{11}

12) $49x^2$

13) $20x^5$

14) $12x^4$

15) $27x^6$

16) $14x^8$

17) $2x^8$

18) $9x^4$

19) $12x^7$

20) $36x^4y$

21) $8x^5y^5$

22) $12x^7y^9$

23) $36x^7y^3$

24) $110x^8y^4$

25) $81x^9y^6$

26) $72x^5y^7$

27) $99x^4y^7$

28) $48x^5y^{10}$

29) $40x^3y^{10}$

30) $42x^6y^5$

31) $72x^7y^8$

32) $198x^{10}y^5$

Zero and Negative Exponents

1) 1

2) $\frac{1}{16}$

3) $\frac{1}{32}$

4) 1

5) $\frac{1}{9}$

6) $\frac{1}{128}$

7) $\frac{1}{169}$

8) $\frac{1}{196}$

9) $\frac{1}{256}$

10) $\frac{1}{400}$

11) $\frac{1}{19}$

12) $\frac{1}{729}$

13) $\frac{1}{225}$

14) $\frac{1}{100}$

15) $\frac{1}{256}$

16) $\frac{1}{900}$

17) $\frac{1}{4,096}$

18) $\frac{1}{2,187}$

19) $\frac{1}{1,024}$

20) $\frac{1}{1,000}$

21) $\frac{1}{324}$

22) $\frac{1}{625}$

23) $\frac{1}{1,600}$

24) $\frac{1}{2,500}$

25) $\frac{1}{1,331}$

26) $\frac{1}{484}$

27) $\frac{1}{289}$

28) $\frac{1}{6,561}$

29) $\frac{1}{1,024}$

30) $\frac{1}{3,600}$

31)

32)

33)

34) 6.25

35) 225

36) $\frac{144}{49}$

37) 400

38) 343

39) $\frac{243}{32}$

40) $\frac{11}{9}$

41) $\frac{81}{64}$

42) 512

Division Property of Exponents

1) $\frac{1}{5^4}$

2) 6^4

3) 9^6

4) $\frac{1}{3^2}$

5) $\frac{2}{x^7}$

6) $\frac{1}{4}$

7) 12^4

8) 7^4

9) 1

10) $\frac{1}{2x^3}$

11) $\frac{8x^3}{9}$

12) $\frac{3}{2x^2}$

13) $\frac{x^2}{2y^8}$

14) $\frac{5y^3}{x^3}$

15) $\frac{2x^6}{3}$

16) $\frac{3y^4}{x^3}$

17) $\frac{2}{x^3y^{14}}$

18) $\frac{6}{x}$ 19) $\frac{1}{2x^3 y^2}$ 20) $\frac{1}{9}$ 21) $\frac{9}{11x^4}$

Powers of Products and Quotients

1) 4^6
2) 5^4
3) 3^9
4) 24^2
5) 15^{20}
6) 7^{20}
7) 9^6
8) 4^{18}
9) $343x^{21}$
10) $64x^8 y^6$
11) $81x^{12} y^8$

12) $16x^4 y^4$
13) $27x^{15} y^6$
14) $64x^9 y^6$
15) $32x^{20}$
16) $36x^{12}$
17) $49x^{24} y^{10}$
18) $125x^{33}$
19) $2,304x^6$
20) $729x^{42} y^9$
21) $625x^{16} y^9$
22) $243x^{15} y^8$

23) $256x^2 y^6$
24) $\frac{512}{x^6}$
25) x^7
26) $\frac{36y^2}{x^8}$
27) $\frac{1}{x^3 y^6}$
28) $x^6 y^{18}$
29) $\frac{125y^{21}}{x^3}$
30) $\frac{64}{y^{12}}$

Negative Exponents and Negative Bases

1) $-\frac{1}{16}$
2) $-\frac{1}{7}$
3) $-\frac{1}{25}$
4) $-\frac{1}{x^9}$
5) $\frac{10}{x^2}$
6) $-\frac{7}{x^4}$
7) $-\frac{15}{x^4}$
8) $-\frac{15}{x^7 y^4}$
9) $\frac{32}{x^9 y^3}$
10) $\frac{45}{a^7 b^3}$

11) $-\frac{25x^3}{y^5}$
12) $-18x^9$
13) $-13xa^8$
14) 81
15) $-\frac{64}{27}$
16) $-12a^6 b^4$
17) $-48x^7$
18) $-\frac{b^5}{a^{12}}$
19) $-27x^5$
20) $-\frac{bc^6}{4}$
21) $24a^5 b^4$

22) $-\frac{p^9}{5n^7}$
23) $-\frac{9ac^2}{5b^6}$
24) $\frac{81c^4}{16a^4}$
25) $\frac{25y^2 z^2}{64x^2}$
26) $-\frac{9ac^3}{4b^6}$
27) $-x^5$
28) $-27x^{18}$
29) $-x^{30}$

Writing Scientific Notation

1) 2.26×10^{-1}
2) 5×10^{-2}
3) 4.8×10^0

4) 9×10^1
5) 1.2×10^2
6) 1.23×10^{-1}

7) 8.2×10^1
8) 5.4×10^3
9) 2.46×10^3

10) 7.53×10^4

11) 61×10^6

12) 9×10^{-5}

13) 4.68×10^5

14) 4.58×10^{-3}

15) 8.7×10^{-5}

16) 3.18×10^7

17) 9.5×10^5

18) 9×10^9

19) 7×10^{-4}

20) 4.1×10^{-4}

21) 0.04

22) 0.0007

23) 4,300,000

24) 0.0007

25) 0.0087

26) 1,200,000

27) 35,000

28) 189,000

29) 0.000013

30) 0.00073

Square Roots

1) 8

2) 2

3) 17

4) 0.5

5) 0.1

6) 0.3

7) 40

8) 1.5

9) 0

10) 0.2

11) 0.6

12) 0.9

13) 0.7

14) 1.1

15) 1.3

16) 0.4

17) 23

18) 25

19) 0.9

20) $2\sqrt{5}$

21) $5\sqrt{2}$

22) 26

23) $3\sqrt{30}$

24) $4\sqrt{2}$

25) 8

26) 56

27) 4

28) 17

29) 13

30) 15

31) $2\sqrt{19}$

32) 2

33) $6\sqrt{7}$

34) 420

35) 90

36) $6\sqrt{3}$

Simplifying radical expressions

1) $y\sqrt{13}$

2) $2x\sqrt{15x}$

3) $3\sqrt[3]{a}$

4) $9x$

5) $5\sqrt{6a}$

6) $3w\sqrt[3]{5}$

7) $10\sqrt{2x}$

8) $8\sqrt{3v}$

9) $4\sqrt[3]{x}$

10) $2x\sqrt{21x}$

11) $11x$

12) $2\sqrt[3]{6a}$

13) $4\sqrt{30}$

14) $15p\sqrt{7}$

15) $6m^3\sqrt{3}$

16) $3x \cdot y\sqrt{22x}$

17) $13xy\sqrt{y}$

18) $5a^3$

19) $5xy\sqrt{2y}$

20) $8y$

21) $24x$

22) $60x$

23) $3y\sqrt[3]{7xy}$

24) $11xy\sqrt[3]{y^2}$

25) $15\sqrt{6a}$

26) $9\sqrt[3]{y}$

27) $9r\sqrt{2xyr}$

28) $90xz^3\sqrt{y}$

29) $15x\sqrt[3]{y^2}$

30) $14ac^2\sqrt{b}$

31) $40x^3y^{15}$

Chapter 5:

Algebraic Expressions

Topics that you will practice in this chapter:

- ✓ Simplifying Variable Expressions
- ✓ Simplifying Polynomial Expressions
- ✓ Translate Phrases into an Algebraic Statement
- ✓ The Distributive Property
- ✓ Evaluating One Variable Expressions
- ✓ Evaluating Two Variables Expressions
- ✓ Combining like Terms

Mathematics is, as it were, a sensuous logic, and relates to philosophy as do the arts, music, and plastic art to poetry. — K. Shegel

Simplifying Variable Expressions

✎ **Simplify each expression.**

1) $3(x + 8) =$

2) $(-4)(7x - 3) =$

3) $11x + 8 - 7x =$

4) $-6 - 2x^2 - 9x^2 =$

5) $8 + 17x^2 + 6 =$

6) $9x^2 + 13x + 19x^2 =$

7) $7x^2 - 15x^2 + 3x =$

8) $8x^2 - 11x - 3x =$

9) $3x + 9(1 - 4x) =$

10) $14x + 2(20x - 4) =$

11) $6(-3x - 7) - 22 =$

12) $7x^2 + (-12x) =$

13) $x - 8 + 15 - 7x =$

14) $3 - 6x + 12 - 3x =$

15) $20x - 14 + 27 + 12x =$

16) $(-7)(6x - 5) + 14x =$

17) $11x - 4(3 - 7x) =$

18) $22x + 3(5x + 2) + 11 =$

19) $4(-3x + 8) + 10x =$

20) $16x - 3x(2x + 7) =$

21) $9x + 12x(2 - 4x) =$

22) $5x(-4x + 11) + 18x =$

23) $20x + 24x + 3x^2 =$

24) $7x(x - 7) - 28 =$

25) $7x - 12 + 5x + 3x^2 =$

26) $4x^2 - 9x - 12x =$

27) $8x - 22x^2 - 21x^2 - 11 =$

28) $9 + 3x^2 - 8x^2 - 27x =$

29) $14x + 2x^2 + 4x + 28 =$

30) $7x^2 + 45x + 12x^2 =$

31) $25 + 15x^2 + 9x - 3x^2 =$

32) $17x - 32x - 2x^2 + 30 =$

Simplifying Polynomial Expressions

✎ **Simplify each polynomial.**

1) $(5x^4 + 2x^2) - (11x + 6x^2) = $ _____

2) $(x^7 + 6x^4) - (8x^4 + 4x^2) = $ _____

3) $(24x^5 + 8x^3) - (x^3 - 12x^5) = $ _____

4) $14x - 9x^5 - 4(7x^5 + 7x^3) = $ _____

5) $(7x^4 - 5) + 2(4x^2 - 8x^4) = $ _____

6) $(9x^5 - 3x) - 3(8x^5 - 3x^4) = $ _____

7) $4(2x - 4x^4) - 5(3x^4 + x^2) = $ _____

8) $(4x^2 - 2x) - (5x^3 + 9x^2) = $ _____

9) $8x^4 - (9x^6 + 2x) + 2x^2 = $ _____

10) $x^5 - 3(x^3 + 2x) + 9x = $ _____

11) $(4x^2 - 2x^5) - (4x^5 - 2x^2) = $ _____

12) $8x^3 - 8x^5 + 17x^4 - 12x^5 = $ _____

13) $4x^3 - 9x^7 + 18x^7 - 24x^6 = $ _____

14) $4x^5 + 13x^3 - 17x^5 + 24x = $ _____

15) $7x^6 - 9x^7 + 5x^6 - 12x^3 = $ _____

16) $4x^4 + 19x - 3x^3 - 21x^4 = $ _____

Translate Phrases into an Algebraic Statement

✍ **Write an algebraic expression for each phrase.**

1) 13 multiplied by x. _____

2) Subtract 15 from y. _____

3) 22 divided by x. _____

4) 27 decreased by y. _____

5) Add y to 31. _____

6) The square of 7. _____

7) x raised to the seventh power. _____

8) The sum of five and a number. _____

9) The difference between forty–nine and y. _____

10) The quotient of eight and a number. _____

11) The quotient of the square of x and 34. _____

12) The difference between x and 14 is 41. _____

13) 7 times b reduced by the square of a. _____

14) Subtract the product of a and b from 51. _____

The Distributive Property

✏ **Use the distributive property to simply each expression.**

1) $4(2 + 5x) =$

2) $5(2 + 4x) =$

3) $6(5x - 5) =$

4) $(6x - 3)(-7) =$

5) $(-4)(x + 8) =$

6) $(4 + 4x)6 =$

7) $(-5)(8 - 7x) =$

8) $-(-3 - 12x) =$

9) $(-8x + 3)(-5) =$

10) $(-5)(x - 11) =$

11) $-(8 - 2x) =$

12) $3(7 + 4x) =$

13) $4(8 + 3x) =$

14) $(-8x + 2)5 =$

15) $(4 - 7x)(-9) =$

16) $(-12)(3x + 5) =$

17) $(9 - 3x)5 =$

18) $4(4 + 7x) =$

19) $12(3x - 6) =$

20) $(-7x + 5)4 =$

21) $(4 - 9x)(-2) =$

22) $(-15)(2x - 3) =$

23) $(14 - 3x)3 =$

24) $(-5)(10x - 4) =$

25) $(5 - 7x)(-12) =$

26) $(-8)(2x + 9) =$

27) $(-5 + 8x)(-7) =$

28) $(-6)(2 - 15x) =$

29) $13(4x - 6) =$

30) $(-15x + 13)(-4) =$

31) $(-9)(3x - 2) + 2(x + 5) =$

32) $(-9)(2x + 2) - (7 + 4x) =$

Evaluating One Variable Expressions

✎ **Evaluate each expression using the value given.**

1) $8 - x, x = 5$

2) $x - 10, x = 6$

3) $3x - 6, x = 5$

4) $x - 15, x = -2$

5) $12 - x, x = 4$

6) $x + 7, x = 1$

7) $2x + 9, x = 7$

8) $x + (-4), x = -7$

9) $2x + 9, x = 4$

10) $3x + 10, x = -2$

11) $18 + 2x - 4, x = -1$

12) $18 - 6x, x = 2$

13) $8x - 2, x = 4$

14) $2x - 17, x = 8$

15) $13x - 12, x = 3$

16) $8 - 5x, x = -2$

17) $3(5x + 4), x = 5$

18) $4(-2x - 7), x = 3$

19) $7x - 5x + 12, x = 2$

20) $(8x + 4) \div 2, x = 6$

21) $(x + 15) \div 4, x = 9$

22) $6x - 10 + 3x, x = -5$

23) $(7 - 4x)(-3), x = -3$

24) $12x^2 + 5x - 4, x = 2$

25) $x^2 - 15x, x = -4$

26) $3x(3 - 6x), x = 2$

27) $13x + 8 - 6x^2, x = -3$

28) $(-2)(15x - 11 + 4x), x = 4$

29) $(-6) + \frac{x}{6} + x, x = 18$

30) $(-9) + \frac{x}{4}, x = 32$

31) $\left(-\frac{45}{x}\right) - 5 + 2x, x = 9$

32) $\left(-\frac{36}{x}\right) - 9 + 3x, x = 3$

Evaluating Two Variables Expressions

✏ **Evaluate each expression using the values given.**

1) $5x - y$,

   $x = 4, y = 3$

2) $3x + 2y$,

   $x = -2, y = 2$

3) $-6a + 5b$,

   $a = 3, b = 1$

4) $3x + 7 - y$,

   $x = 8, y = 4$

5) $5z + 12 - 3k$,

   $z = 5 , k = 2$

6) $6 (-x - 3y)$,

   $x = 5, y = 4$

7) $7a + 4b$,

   $a = 3, b = 5$

8) $8x \div 4y$,

   $x = 6, y = 4$

9) $2x + 18 + 4y$,

   $x = -3, y = 3$

10) $5a - (18 - 2b)$,

   $a = 5, b = 8$

11) $6z + 12 + 3k$,

   $z = -3, k = 3$

12) $2xy + 6 + 7x$,

   $x = 5, y = 3$

13) $6x + 2y - 9 + 3$,

   $x = 3, y = 2$

14) $\left(-\frac{21}{x}\right) + 6 + 3y$,

   $x = 7, y = 4$

15) $(-4) (- 3a - b)$,

   $a = 2, b = 6$

16) $18 + 4x + 9 - 5y$,

   $x = 6, y = 4$

17) $7x + 5 - 6y + 11$,

   $x = 9, y = 3$

18) $9 + 4(-5x - 3y)$,

   $x = 4, y = 5$

19) $3x + 15 + 6y$,

   $x = 2, y = 4$

20) $7a - (4a - 2b) + 8$,

   $a = 3, b = 1$

Combining like Terms

✍ **Simplify each expression.**

1) $7x + 2x + 8 =$

2) $3(6x - 2) =$

3) $10x - 12x + 8 =$

4) $20x - 32x + 14 =$

5) $16x - 6x - 12 =$

6) $18x - 21 + 4x =$

7) $15 - (3x + 9) =$

8) $-14x + 7 - 11x =$

9) $5x - 10 - 3x + 1 =$

10) $24x + 7x - 22 =$

11) $14x + 8x - 2 =$

12) $(-4x + 2)8 =$

13) $34 + 6x + 8x - 4 =$

14) $3(x - 8x) - 5 =$

15) $4(2x + 7) + 5x =$

16) $x - 27 - 9x =$

17) $3(5 + 4x) - 8x =$

18) $41x + 24 + 3x =$

19) $(-8x) + 30 + 15x =$

20) $(-4x) - 12 + 19x =$

21) $5(2x + 6) + 9x =$

22) $3(6 - 7x) - 11x =$

23) $-8x - (16 - 14x) =$

24) $(-9) - (6)(5x + 9) =$

25) $(-4)(6x - 5) - 12x =$

26) $-34x + 14 + 9x - 21x =$

27) $5(-13x + 6) - 24x =$

28) $-7x - 20 + 15x =$

29) $42x - 31x + 15 - 12x =$

30) $4(8x + 5x) - 17 =$

31) $54 - 22x - 28 - 19x =$

32) $-9(-7x - 11x) + 58x =$

Answers of Worksheets – Chapter 5

Simplifying Variable Expressions

1) $3x + 24$

2) $-28x + 12$

3) $4x + 8$

4) $-11x^2 - 6$

5) $17x^2 + 14$

6) $28x^2 + 13x$

7) $-8x^2 + 3x$

8) $8x^2 - 14x$

9) $-33x + 9$

10) $54x - 8$

11) $-18x - 64$

12) $7x^2 - 12x$

13) $-6x + 7$

14) $-9x + 15$

15) $32x + 13$

16) $-28x + 35$

17) $39x - 12$

18) $37x + 17$

19) $-2x + 32$

20) $-6x^2 - 5x$

21) $-48x^2 + 33x$

22) $-20x^2 + 73x$

23) $3x^2 + 44x$

24) $7x^2 - 49x - 28$

25) $3x^2 + 12x - 12$

26) $4x^2 - 21x$

27) $-43x^2 + 8x - 11$

28) $-5x^2 - 27x + 9$

29) $2x^2 + 18x + 28$

30) $19x^2 + 45x$

31) $12x^2 + 9x + 25$

32) $-2x^2 - 15x + 30$

Simplifying Polynomial Expressions

1) $5x^4 - 4x^2 - 11x$

2) $x^7 - 2x^4 - 4x^2$

3) $36x^5 + 7x^3$

4) $-37x^5 - 28x^2 + 14x$

5) $-9x^4 + 8x^2 - 5$

6) $-15x^5 + 9x^4 - 3x$

7) $-31x^3 - 5x^2 + 8x$

8) $-5x^3 - 5x^2 - 2x$

9) $-9x^6 + 8x^4 + 2x^2 - 2x$

10) $x^5 - 3x^3 + 3x$

11) $-6x^5 + 6x^2$

12) $-20x^5 + 17x^4 + 8x^3$

13) $9x^7 - 24x^6 + 4x^3$

14) $-13x^5 + 13x^3 + 24x$

15) $-9x^7 + 12x^6 - 12x^3$

16) $-17x^4 - 3x^3 + 19x$

Translate Phrases into an Algebraic Statement

1) $13x$

2) $y - 15$

3) $\frac{22}{x}$

4) $27 - y$

5) $y + 31$

6) 7^2

7) x^7

8) $5 + x$

9) $49 - y$

10) $\frac{8}{x}$

11) $\frac{x^2}{34}$

12) $x - 14 = 41$

13) $7b - a^2$

14) $51 - ab$

The Distributive Property

1) $20x + 8$

2) $20x + 10$

3) $30x - 30$

4) $-42x + 21$

5) $-4x - 32$

6) $24x + 24$

7) $35x - 40$

8) $12x + 3$

9) $40x - 15$

10) $-5x + 55$

11) $2x - 8$

12) $12x + 21$

13) $12x + 32$	18) $28x + 16$	23) $-9x + 42$	28) $90x - 12$
14) $-40x + 10$	19) $36x - 72$	24) $-50x + 20$	29) $52x - 78$
15) $63x - 36$	20) $-28x + 20$	25) $84x - 60$	30) $60x - 52$
16) $-36x - 60$	21) $18x - 8$	26) $-16x - 72$	31) $-25x + 28$
17) $-15x + 45$	22) $-30x + 45$	27) $56x - 35$	32) $-22x - 25$

Evaluating One Variables

1) 3	9) 17	17) 87	25) 76
2) −4	10) 4	18) −52	26) −54
3) 9	11) 12	19) 16	27) −85
4) −17	12) 6	20) 26	28) −130
5) 8	13) 30	21) 6	29) 15
6) 8	14) −1	22) −55	30) −1
7) 23	15) 27	23) −57	31) 8
8) − 11	16) 18	24) 54	32) −12

Evaluating Two Variables

1) 17	6) −102	11) 3	16) 31
2) −2	7) 41	12) 71	17) 61
3) −13	8) 3	13) 16	18) −131
4) 27	9) 24	14) 15	19) 45
5) 31	10) 23	15) 48	20) 19

Combining like Terms

1) $9x + 8$	9) $2x - 9$	17) $4x + 15$	25) $-36x + 20$
2) $18x - 6$	10) $31x - 22$	18) $44x + 24$	26) $-46x + 14$
3) $-2x + 8$	11) $22x - 2$	19) $7x + 30$	27) $-89x + 30$
4) $-12x + 14$	12) $-32x + 16$	20) $15x - 12$	28) $8x - 20$
5) $10x - 12$	13) $14x + 30$	21) $19x + 30$	29) $-x + 15$
6) $22x - 22$	14) $-21x - 5$	22) $-32x + 18$	30) $52x - 17$
7) $-3x + 6$	15) $13x + 28$	23) $6x - 16$	31) $-41x + 26$
8) $-25x + 7$	16) $-8x - 27$	24) $-30x - 63$	32) $220x$

Chapter 6:

Equations and Inequalities

Topics that you will practice in this chapter:

- ✓ One–Step Equations
- ✓ Multi–Step Equations
- ✓ Graphing Single–Variable Inequalities
- ✓ One–Step Inequalities
- ✓ Multi-Step Inequalities
- ✓ Systems of Equations
- ✓ Systems of Equations Word Problems

"Life is a math equation. In order to gain the most, you have to know how to convert negatives into positives." – Anonymous

One–Step Equations

✍ **Find the answer for each equation.**

1) $3x = 90, x =$ ____

2) $5x = 35, x =$ ____

3) $9x = 36, x =$ ____

4) $25x = 150, x =$ ____

5) $x + 18 = 23, x =$ ____

6) $x - 3 = 8, x =$ ____

7) $x - 7 = 4, x =$ ____

8) $x + 22 = 30, x =$ ____

9) $x - 11 = 6, x =$ ____

10) $24 = 28 + x, x =$ ____

11) $x - 5 = 7, x =$ ____

12) $9 - x = -7, x =$ ____

13) $43 = -8 + x, x =$ ____

14) $x - 23 = -38, x =$ ____

15) $x + 45 = -27, x =$ ____

16) $42 = 56 - x, x =$ ____

17) $-18 + x = -32, x =$ ____

18) $x - 13 = 7, x =$ ____

19) $35 = x - 10, x =$ ____

20) $x - 8 = -21, x =$ ____

21) $x - 54 = -20, x =$ ____

22) $x - 42 = -47, x =$ ____

23) $x - 8 = 29, x =$ ____

24) $-93 = x - 51, x =$ ____

25) $x + 15 = 37, x =$ ____

26) $108 = 12x, x =$ ____

27) $x - 33 = 27, x =$ ____

28) $x - 12 = 23, x =$ ____

29) $72 - x = 18, x =$ ____

30) $x + 34 = 58, x =$ ____

31) $21 - x = -9, x =$ __

32) $x - 59 = -80, x =$ ____

Multi–Step Equations

✎ **Find the answer for each equation.**

1) $3x + 1 = 7$

2) $-x + 10 = 9$

3) $5x - 13 = 7$

4) $-(4 - x) = 5$

5) $3x - 8 = 16$

6) $15x - 13 = 17$

7) $3x - 28 = 2$

8) $9x + 21 = 39$

9) $14x + 17 = 45$

10) $-14(8 + x) = 70$

11) $8(10 + x) = 32$

12) $16 = -(x - 8)$

13) $5(7 - 3x) = 50$

14) $-19 = -(3x + 7)$

15) $30(3 + x) = 60$

16) $9(x - 12) = 54$

17) $-24 = 3x + 5x$

18) $5x + 28 = -2x - 7$

19) $9(5 + 4x) = -99$

20) $18 - x = -12 - 6x$

21) $4 - 4x = 28 - 2x$

22) $15 + 12x = -15 + 8x$

23) $54 = (-3x) - 8 + 8$

24) $12 = 7x - 18 + 5x$

25) $-18 = -9x - 42 + 5x$

26) $11x - 6 = -33 + 8x$

27) $8x - 42 = 3x + 3$

28) $-15 - 8x = 4(5 - x)$

29) $x - 9 = -5(9 - 2x)$

30) $14x - 65 = -x - 110$

31) $3x - 129 = -3(11 + 7x)$

32) $-7x - 20 = 2x + 43$

Graphing Single–Variable Inequalities

 Draw a graph for each inequality.

1) $x \leq 7$

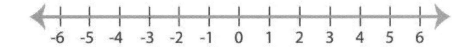

2) $x \leq -1.5$

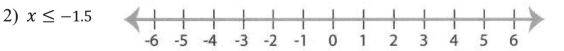

3) $x < -4$

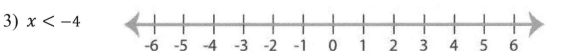

4) $x > 2.5$

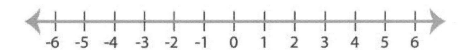

5) $x > 1.3$

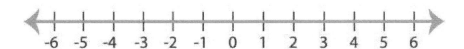

6) $x < 4$

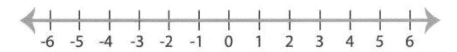

7) $x < 2.4$

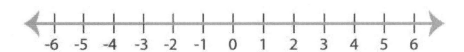

8) $x > -\dfrac{18}{10}$

One–Step Inequalities

✎ **Find the answer for each inequality and graph it.**

1) $x + 3 > -5$

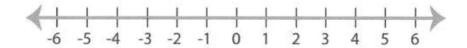

2) $x - 4 < 1$

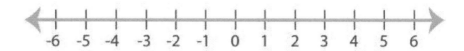

3) $7x < 42$

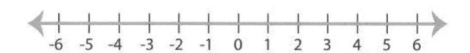

4) $13 + x > 12$

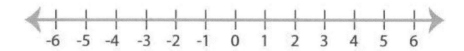

5) $x + 20 < 13$

6) $14x \leq 42$

7) $11x \leq -44$

8) $x + 26 > 35$

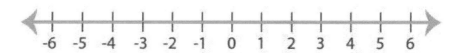

Multi-Step Inequalities

✎ **Calculate each inequality.**

1) $x - 8 \leq 12$

2) $9 - 3x \leq 18$

3) $4x - 7 \leq 9$

4) $8x - 9 \geq 15$

5) $x - 19 \geq 24$

6) $5x - 15 \leq 40$

7) $7x - 4 \leq 24$

8) $-18 + 8x \leq 22$

9) $9(x - 8) \leq 27$

10) $4x - 8 \leq 16$

11) $11x - 42 < 22$

12) $10x - 18 < 52$

13) $17 - 9x \geq -46$

14) $32 + 2x < 68$

15) $8 + 8x \geq 80$

16) $11 + 6x < 65$

17) $9x - 13 < 23$

18) $8(12 - 4x) \geq -68$

19) $-(2 + 5x) < 42$

20) $14 - 9x \geq -31$

21) $-5(x - 3) > 65$

22) $\dfrac{2x + 8}{3} \leq 12$

23) $\dfrac{8x + 16}{4} \leq 24$

24) $\dfrac{2x - 22}{9} > 8$

25) $7 + \dfrac{x}{4} < 21$

26) $\dfrac{32x}{16} - 4 < 6$

27) $\dfrac{12x + 36}{22} > 3$

28) $42 + \dfrac{x}{3} < 15$

Systems of Equations

✎ **Calculate each system of equations.**

1) $-6x + 7y = 8$ $x = \underline{\quad}$
    $x + 4y = 9$ $y = \underline{\quad}$

2) $-4x + 12y = 12$ $x = \underline{\quad}$
    $14x - 16y = 10$ $y = \underline{\quad}$

3) $y = -9$ $x = \underline{\quad}$
    $2x - 5y = 12$ $y = \underline{\quad}$

4) $4y = -4x + 20$ $x = \underline{\quad}$
    $8x - 2y = -12$ $y = \underline{\quad}$

5) $10x - 9y = -13$ $x = \underline{\quad}$
    $-5x + 3y = 11$ $y = \underline{\quad}$

6) $-6x - 8y = 10$ $x = \underline{\quad}$
    $4x - 8y = 20$ $y = \underline{\quad}$

7) $5x - 14y = -23$ $x = \underline{\quad}$
    $-6x + 7y = 8$ $y = \underline{\quad}$

8) $-4x + 3y = 3$ $x = \underline{\quad}$
    $-x + 2y = 5$ $y = \underline{\quad}$

9) $-4x + 5y = 15$ $x = \underline{\quad}$
    $-3x + 4y = -10$ $y = \underline{\quad}$

10) $-6x - 6y = -21$ $x = \underline{\quad}$
    $-6x + 6y = -66$ $y = \underline{\quad}$

11) $12x - 21y = 6$ $x = \underline{\quad}$
    $-6x - 3y = -12$ $y = \underline{\quad}$

12) $-4x - 4y = -14$ $x = \underline{\quad}$
    $4x - 4y = 44$ $y = \underline{\quad}$

13) $4x + 5y = 3$ $x = \underline{\quad}$
    $3x - y = 6$ $y = \underline{\quad}$

14) $3x - 2y = 2$ $x = \underline{\quad}$
    $10x - 10y = 20$ $y = \underline{\quad}$

15) $5x + 8y = 14$ $x = \underline{\quad}$
    $-3x - 2y = -3$ $y = \underline{\quad}$

16) $8x + 5y = 4$ $x = \underline{\quad}$
    $-3x - 4y = 15$ $y = \underline{\quad}$

Systems of Equations Word Problems

✎ **Find the answer for each word problem.**

1) Tickets to a movie cost $6 for adults and $4 for students. A group of friends purchased 9 tickets for $50.00. How many adults ticket did they buy? ____

2) At a store, Eva bought two shirts and five hats for $77.00. Nicole bought three same shirts and four same hats for $84.00. What is the price of each shirt? ____

3) A farmhouse shelters 10 animals, some are pigs, and some are ducks. Altogether there are 36 legs. How many pigs are there? ____

4) A class of 85 students went on a field trip. They took 24 vehicles, some cars and some buses. If each car holds 3 students and each bus hold 16 students, how many buses did they take? ____

5) A theater is selling tickets for a performance. Mr. Smith purchased 8 senior tickets and 10 child tickets for $248 for his friends and family. Mr. Jackson purchased 4 senior tickets and 6 child tickets for $132. What is the price of a senior ticket? $____

6) The difference of two numbers is 15. Their sum is 33. What is the bigger number? $____

7) The sum of the digits of a certain two–digit number is 7. Reversing its digits increase the number by 9. What is the number? ____

8) The difference of two numbers is 11. Their sum is 25. What are the numbers? _____

9) The length of a rectangle is 5 meters greater than 2 times the width. The perimeter of rectangle is 28 meters. What is the length of the rectangle? _____

10) Jim has 23 nickels and dimes totaling $2.40. How many nickels does he have? ____

Answers of Worksheets – Chapter 6

One–Step Equations

1) 30	9) 17	17) −14	25) 22
2) 7	10) −4	18) 20	26) 9
3) 4	11) 12	19) 45	27) 60
4) 6	12) 16	20) −13	28) 35
5) 5	13) 51	21) 34	29) 54
6) 11	14) −15	22) −5	30) 24
7) 11	15) −72	23) 37	31) 30
8) 8	16) 14	24) −42	32) −21

Multi–Step Equations

1) 2	9) 2	17) −3	25) −6
2) 1	10) −13	18) −5	26) −9
3) 4	11) −6	19) −4	27) 9
4) 9	12) −8	20) −6	28) −8.75
5) 8	13) −1	21) −12	29) 4
6) 2	14) 4	22) −7.5	30) −3
7) 10	15) −1	23) −18	31) 4
8) 2	16) 18	24) 2.5	32) −7

Graphing Single–Variable Inequalities

1)

2)

3)

4)

5)

6)

7)

8)

One–Step Inequalities

1)

2)

3)

4)

5)

6)

7)

8)

Multi-Step Inequalities

1) $x \leq 20$	5) $x \geq 43$	9) $x \leq 11$	13) $x \leq 7$
2) $x \geq -3$	6) $x \leq 11$	10) $x \leq 6$	14) $x < 18$
3) $x \leq 4$	7) $x \leq 4$	11) $x < 64/11$	15) $x \geq 9$
4) $x \geq 3$	8) $x \leq 5$	12) $x < 7$	16) $x < 9$

17) $x < 4$

18) $x \le 41/8$

19) $x > -44/5$

20) $x \le 5$

21) $x < -10$

22) $x \le 14$

23) $x \le 10$

24) $x > 47$

25) $x < 56$

26) $x < 9/4$

27) $x > 2.5$

28) $x < -81$

Systems of Equations

1) $x = 1, y = 2$

2) $x = 3, y = 2$

3) $x = -\frac{33}{2}$

4) $x = -\frac{1}{5}, y = \frac{26}{5}$

5) $x = -4, y = -3$

6) $x = 1, y = -2$

7) $x = 1, y = 2$

8) $x = \frac{9}{5}, y = \frac{17}{5}$

9) $x = -110, y = -85$

10) $x = -\frac{15}{4}, y = \frac{29}{4}$

11) $x = \frac{5}{3}, y = \frac{2}{3}$

12) $x = -\frac{15}{4}, y = \frac{29}{4}$

13) $x = \frac{33}{19}, y = -\frac{15}{19}$

14) $x = -2, y = -4$

15) $x = -\frac{2}{7}, y = \frac{27}{14}$

16) $x = \frac{91}{17}, y = -\frac{132}{17}$

Systems of Equations Word Problems

1) 7

2) $16

3) 8

4) 1

5) $21

6) 24

7) 43

8) 18, 7

9) 11 meters

10) 18

Chapter 7:

Linear Functions

Topics that you will practice in this chapter:

- ✓ Finding Slope
- ✓ Graphing Lines Using Line Equation
- ✓ Writing Linear Equations
- ✓ Graphing Linear Inequalities
- ✓ Finding Midpoint
- ✓ Finding Distance of Two Points

"Nature is written in mathematical language." – Galileo Galilei

Finding Slope

✎ **Find the slope of each line.**

1) $y = 2x + 5$

2) $y = -x + 17$

3) $y = 4x + 16$

4) $y = -3x + 15$

5) $y = 27 + 7x$

6) $y = 11 - 4x$

7) $y = 7x + 14$

8) $y = -8x + 18$

9) $y = -9x + 15$

10) $y = 8x - 13$

11) $y = \frac{1}{5}x + 9$

12) $y = -\frac{3}{7}x + 19$

13) $-3x + 6y = 17$

14) $4x + 4y = 16$

15) $8y - 3x = 32$

16) $11y - 3x = 42$

✎ **Find the slope of the line through each pair of points.**

17) $(1, 8), (5, 16)$

18) $(-2, 14), (2, 18)$

19) $(7, -1), (3, 9)$

20) $(-4, -4), (2, 14)$

21) $(16, -1), (4, 11)$

22) $(-21, 5), (-10, 38)$

23) $(8, 11), (12, 19)$

24) $(22, -22), (10, 14)$

25) $(21, -15), (19, -13)$

26) $(11, 10), (7, -2)$

27) $(5, 4), (9, 16)$

28) $(34, -87), (22, 45)$

Graphing Lines Using Line Equation

✎ **Sketch the graph of each line.**

1) $y = x - 5$

2) $y = -3x + 4$

3) $x - 2y = 0$

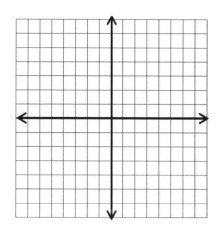
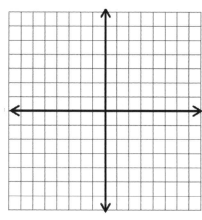
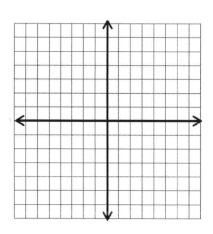

4) $x + y = -4$

5) $4x + 3y = -2$

6) $y - 3x + 6 = 0$

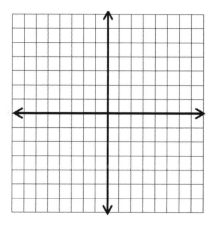
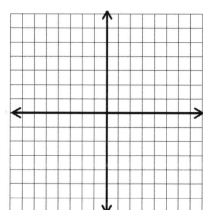
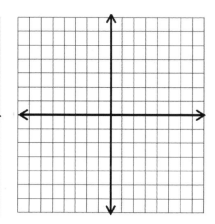

Writing Linear Equations

✍ **Write the equation of the line through the given points.**

1) Through: $(6, -10), (10, 14)$

2) Through: $(10, 4), (4, 22)$

3) Through: $(-6, 4), (2, 12)$

4) Through: $(15, 11), (3, -1)$

5) Through: $(-5, 33), (9, 5)$

6) Through: $(20, 5), (17, 2)$

7) Through: $(24, -4), (16, 4)$

8) Through: $(-18, 57), (33, -45)$

9) Through: $(10, 12), (8, 18)$

10) Through: $(25, 41), (33, -7)$

11) Through: $(-6, 9), (-8, -7)$

12) Through: $(8, 8), (4, -8)$

13) Through: $(6, -10), (10, 6)$

14) Through: $(10, -24), (-8, 12)$

15) Through: $(10, 10), (-2, -4)$

16) Through: $(-7, 35), (11, -31)$

✍ **Find the answer for each problem.**

17) What is the equation of a line with slope3 and intercept 11?

_____

18) What is the equation of a line with slope 5 and intercept 15?

_____

19) What is the equation of a line with slope 7 and passes through point $(3, 2)$? _____

20) What is the equation of a line with slope -3 and passes through point $(-2, 5)$? _____

21) The slope of a line is -6 and it passes through point $(-2, 1)$. What is the equation of the line? _____

22) The slope of a line is 5 and it passes through point $(-4, 2)$. What is the equation of the line? _____

Graphing Linear Inequalities

✎ **Sketch the graph of each linear inequality.**

1) $y > 3x - 5$ 2) $y < 2x + 1$ 3) $y \le -4x - 5$

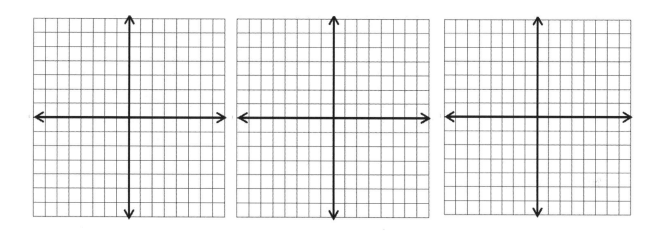

4) $2y \ge 12 + 4x$ 5) $-5y < x - 15$ 6) $3y \ge -9x + 6$

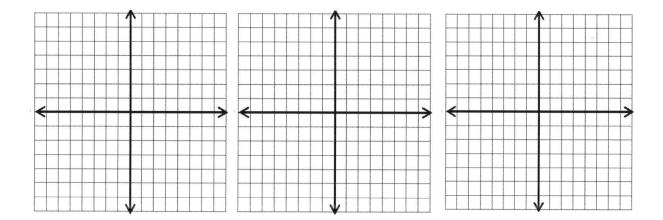

Finding Midpoint

✒ **Find the midpoint of the line segment with the given endpoints.**

1) $(-4, -6), (2, 4)$

2) $(13, 5), (-1, 5)$

3) $(11, -4), (3, 14)$

4) $(-15, -6), (3, 9)$

5) $(7, -8), (13, -12)$

6) $(-14, -8), (8, -12)$

7) $(9, 2), (-9, 22)$

8) $(-8, 10), (-8, 4)$

9) $(-7, 7), (23, -15)$

10) $(3, 17), (19, -5)$

11) $(-4, 13), (7, 9)$

12) $(11, 8), (-3, -6)$

13) $(-4, 12), (0, 6)$

14) $(34, 12), (18, -28)$

15) $(15, 6), (-1, 0)$

16) $(-11, -13), (-13, 19)$

17) $(12, 4), (8, 16)$

18) $(-2, -7), (18, -21)$

19) $(18, 13), (-6, 5)$

20) $(10, -4), (0, 18)$

21) $(4, -4), (8, -20)$

22) $(25, 5), (-11, -17)$

23) $(8, 12), (16, -2)$

24) $(14, -20), (8, 14)$

✒ **Find the answer for each problem.**

25) One endpoint of a line segment is $(6, 8)$ and the midpoint of the line segment is $(1, 6)$. What is the other endpoint? _____

26) One endpoint of a line segment is $(-7, 5)$ and the midpoint of the line segment is $(1, 3)$. What is the other endpoint? _____

27) One endpoint of a line segment is $(-6, -10)$ and the midpoint of the line segment is $(2, 9)$. What is the other endpoint? _____

Finding Distance of Two Points

✎ **Find the distance between each pair of points.**

1) $(5, 9), (-11, -3)$

2) $(-6, 2), (-2, 6)$

3) $(-8, -1), (-3, 8)$

4) $(-8, -2), (2, 22)$

5) $(6, -4), (-12, -28)$

6) $(-6, 0), (-2, 3)$

7) $(8, 12), (8, 6)$

8) $(12, -10), (12, -2)$

9) $(15, 27), (-33, -9)$

10) $(10, -2), (6, -14)$

11) $(1, 0), (6, 12)$

12) $(8, 4), (3, -8)$

13) $(3, 2), (-5, -11)$

14) $(-10, 12), (6, 42)$

15) $(0, 16), (-8, 10)$

16) $(5, 0), (30, 60)$

17) $(3, 5), (-5, -10)$

18) $(-4, 6), (4, 3)$

19) $(7, 2), (-8, -18)$

20) $(-10, 8), (14, 18)$

✎ **Find the answer for each problem.**

21) Triangle ABC is a right triangle on the coordinate system and its vertices are $(-5, 7), (-5, 1),$ and $(1, 1)$. What is the area of triangle ABC?

_____

22) Three vertices of a triangle on a coordinate system are $(1, 1), (7, 1),$ and $(1, 9)$. What is the perimeter of the triangle? _____

23) Four vertices of a rectangle on a coordinate system are $(-2, 4), (-2, 7),$ $(4, 4),$ and $(4, 7)$. What is its perimeter? _____

Answers of Worksheets – Chapter 7

Finding Slope

1) 2

2) -1

3) 4

4) -3

5) 7

6) -4

7) 7

8) -8

9) -9

10) 8

11) $\frac{1}{5}$

12) $-\frac{3}{7}$

13) $\frac{1}{2}$

14) -1

15) $\frac{3}{8}$

16) $\frac{3}{11}$

17) 2

18) 1

19) $-\frac{5}{2}$

20) 3

21) -1

22) 3

23) 2

24) -3

25) -1

26) 3

27) 3

28) -11

Graphing Lines Using Line Equation

1) $y = x - 5$

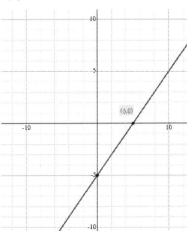

2) $y = -3x + 4$

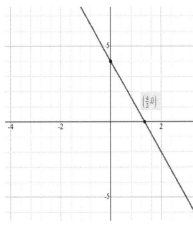

3) $x - 2y = 0$

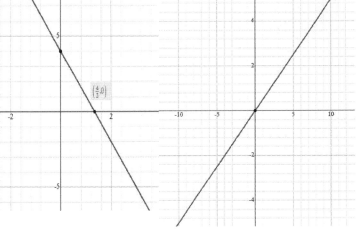

4) $x + y = -4$

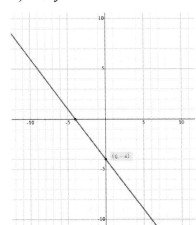

5) $4x + 3y = -2$

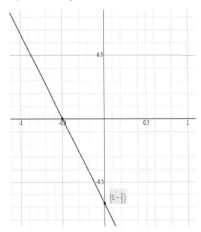

6) $y - 3x + 6 = 0$

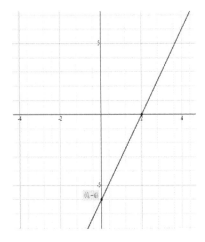

Writing Linear Equations

1) $y = 6x - 46$

2) $y = -3x + 34$

3) $y = x + 10$

4) $y = x - 4$

5) $y = -2x + 23$

6) $y = x - 15$

7) $y = -x + 20$

8) $y = -2x + 21$

9) $y = -3x + 42$

10) $y = -6x + 191$

11) $y = 8x + 57$

12) $y = 4x - 24$

13) $y = 4x - 34$

14) $y = -2x - 4$

15) $y = \frac{7}{6}x - \frac{5}{3}$

16) $y = -\frac{11}{3}x + \frac{28}{3}$

17) $y = 3x + 11$

18) $y = 5x + 15$

19) $y = 7x - 19$

20) $y = -3x - 1$

21) $y = -6x - 11$

22) $y = 5x + 22$

Graphing Linear Inequalities

1) $y > 3x - 5$

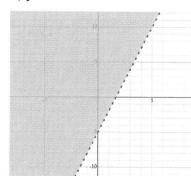

2) $y < 2x + 1$

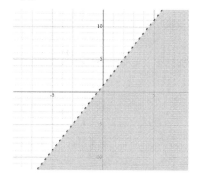

3) $y \leq -4x - 5$

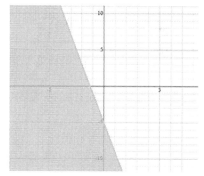

4) $2y \geq 12 + 4x$

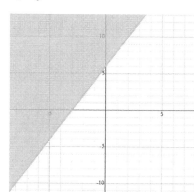

5) $-5y < x - 15$

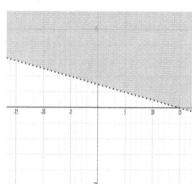

6) $3y \geq -9x + 6$

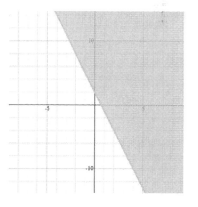

Finding Midpoint

1) $(-1, -1)$

2) $(6, 5)$

3) $(7, 5)$

4) $(-6, 1.5)$

5) $(10, -10)$

6) $(-3, -10)$

7) $(0, 12)$

8) $(-8, 7)$

9) $(8, -4)$

10) $(11, 6)$

11) $(1.5, 11)$

12) $(4, 1)$

13) $(-2, 9)$

14) $(26, -8)$

15) $(7, 3)$

16) $(-12, 3)$

17) $(10, 10)$

18) $(8, -14)$

19) $(6, 9)$

20) $(5, 7)$

21) $(6, -12)$

22) $(7, -6)$

23) $(12, 5)$

24) $(11, -3)$

25) $(-4, 4)$

26) $(9, 1)$

27) $(10, 28)$

Finding Distance of Two Points

1) 20

2) $4\sqrt{2}$

3) $\sqrt{106}$

4) 26

5) 30

6) 10

7) 6

8) 8

9) 60

10) $4\sqrt{10}$

11) 13

12) 13

13) $\sqrt{233}$

14) 34

15) 10

16) 65

17) 17

18) $\sqrt{73}$

19) 25

20) 26

21) 18 square units

22) 24 units

23) 18 units

Chapter 8:

Polynomials

Topics that you will practice in this chapter:

- ✓ Writing Polynomials in Standard Form
- ✓ Simplifying Polynomials
- ✓ Adding and Subtracting Polynomials
- ✓ Multiplying Monomials
- ✓ Multiplying and Dividing Monomials
- ✓ Multiplying a Polynomial and a Monomial
- ✓ Multiplying Binomials
- ✓ Factoring Trinomials
- ✓ Operations with Polynomials

Mathematics is the supreme judge; from its decisions there is no appeal. – Tobias Dantzig

Writing Polynomials in Standard Form

✎ **Write each polynomial in standard form.**

1) $9x - 7x =$

2) $-6 + 15x - 15x =$

3) $3x^2 - 11x^3 =$

4) $18 + 19x^3 - 14 =$

5) $3x^2 + 9x - 4x^5 =$

6) $-7x^3 + 12x^7 =$

7) $9x + 6x^2 - 2x^6 =$

8) $-5x^3 + x - 9x^4 =$

9) $8x^2 + 34 - 21x =$

10) $8 - 7x + 11x^4 =$

11) $25x^3 + 45x - 13x^4 =$

12) $17 + 9x^2 - 2x^3 =$

13) $18x^2 - 8x + 8x^3 =$

14) $9x^4 - 4x^2 - 10x^5 =$

15) $-41 + 7x^2 - 8x^4 =$

16) $8x^2 - 7x^5 + 3x^3 - 12 =$

17) $4x^2 - 9x^5 + 12 - 8x^4 =$

18) $-2x^5 + 6x - 9x^2 - 7x =$

19) $14x^5 + 7x^4 - 8x^5 - 8x^2 =$

20) $2x^3 - 15x^4 + 9x^3 + 3x^8 =$

21) $7x^4 - 16x^5 - 9x^2 + 10x^4 =$

22) $5x^2 + 6x^5 + 37x^3 - 9x^5 =$

23) $3x(2x + 5 - 6x^2) =$

24) $12x(x^6 + 2x^3) =$

25) $6x(x^2 + 8x + 4) =$

26) $8x(3 - 2x + 4x^3) =$

27) $7x(2x^3 - 2x^2 + 2) =$

28) $5x(5x^5 + 4x^4 - 1) =$

29) $x(4x^3 + 52x^4 + 2x) =$

30) $6x(3x - 4x^4 + 7x^2) =$

Simplifying Polynomials

✏️ **Simplify each expression.**

1) $3(x - 12) =$

2) $5x(2x - 4) =$

3) $7x(5x - 1) =$

4) $6x(3x + 2) =$

5) $5x(2x - 7) =$

6) $9x(x + 8) =$

7) $(3x - 8)(x - 3) =$

8) $(x - 9)(3x + 4) =$

9) $(x - 8)(x - 5) =$

10) $(3x + 4)(3x - 4) =$

11) $(5x - 8)(5x - 2) =$

12) $7x^2 + 7x^2 - 6x^4 =$

13) $5x - 2x^2 + 7x^3 + 10 =$

14) $8x + 2x^2 - 5x^3 =$

15) $15x + 4x^5 - 8x^2 =$

16) $-4x^2 + 7x^5 + 11x^4 =$

17) $-14x^2 + 8x^3 - 2x^4 + 5x =$

18) $14 - 5x^2 + 6x^2 - 10x^3 + 17 =$

19) $x^2 - 9x + 2x^3 + 15x - 10x =$

20) $14 - 8x^2 + 4x^2 - 9x^3 + 1 =$

21) $-4x^5 + 2x^4 - 18x^2 + 2x^5 =$

22) $(3x^3 - 5) + (3x^3 - 2x^3) =$

23) $4(3x^5 - 3x^3 - 6x^5) =$

24) $-4(x^5 + 8) - 4(12 - x^5) =$

25) $7x^2 - 9x^3 - 2x + 14 - 5x^2 =$

26) $10 - 5x^2 + 3x^2 - 4x^3 + 4 =$

27) $(8x^2 - 2x) - (5x - 5 - 4x^2) =$

28) $4x^4 - 8x^3 - x(3x^2 + 5x) =$

29) $4x + 8x^2 - 10 - 2(x^2 - 1) =$

30) $5 - 3x^2 + (6x^4 - 2x^2 + 8x^4) =$

31) $-(x^5 + 8) - 7(4 + x^5) =$

32) $(4x^3 - x) - (x - 6x^3) =$

Adding and Subtracting Polynomials

✎ **Add or subtract expressions.**

1) $(-x^3 - 3) + (4x^3 + 2) =$

2) $(3x^2 + 4) - (6 - x^2) =$

3) $(x^3 + 4x^2) - (5x^3 + 15) =$

4) $(3x^3 - 2x^2) + (2x^2 - x) =$

5) $(10x^3 + 14x) - (14x^3 + 7) =$

6) $(5x^2 - 7) + (3x^2 + 7) =$

7) $(9x^3 + 4) - (10 - 5x^3) =$

8) $(x^2 + 2x^3) - (2x^3 + 5) =$

9) $(8x^2 - x) + (5x - 4x^2) =$

10) $(17x + 10) - (2x + 10) =$

11) $(12x^4 - 4x) - (x - 3x^4) =$

12) $(3x - x^4) - (7x^4 + 8x) =$

13) $(7x^3 - 6x^5) - (4x^5 - 2x) =$

14) $(x^3 - 7) + (4x^3 + 8x^5) =$

15) $(6x^2 + 5x^4) - (x^4 - 9x^2) =$

16) $(-4x^2 - 4x) + (7x - 8x^2) =$

17) $(x - 6x^4) - (15x^4 + 2x) =$

18) $(4x - 3x^4) - (2x^4 - 3x^3) =$

19) $(7x^3 - 7) + (6x^3 - 6x^2) =$

20) $(9x^5 + 7x^4) - (x^4 - 5x^5) =$

21) $(-4x^2 + 11x^4 + 2x^3) + (20x^3 + 4x^4 + 12x^2) =$

22) $(5x^2 - 5x^4 - 5x) - (-4x^2 - 5x^4 + 5x) =$

23) $(12x + 36x^3 - 10x^4) + (20x^3 + 10x^4 - 7x) =$

24) $(2x^5 - 4x^3 - 5x) - (2x^2 + 7x^3 - 2x) =$

25) $(14x^3 - 4x^5 - x) - (-4x^3 - 12x^5 + 9x) =$

26) $(-5x^2 + 12x^4 + x^3) + (10x^3 + 17x^4 + 7x^2) =$

Multiplying Monomials

✍ **Simplify each expression.**

1) $7u^5 \times (-u^2) =$

2) $(-9p^8) \times (-4p^2) =$

3) $5xy^3z^3 \times 4z^2 =$

4) $8u^6t \times 2ut^2 =$

5) $(-2a^2) \times (-5a^3b^3) =$

6) $-4a^2b^2 \times 5a^4b =$

7) $10xy^4 \times 2x^2y^2 =$

8) $4p^2q^4 \times (-2pq^2) =$

9) $8s^5t^4 \times 3st^4 =$

10) $(-7x^5y^3) \times 7x^4y =$

11) $xy^7z \times 15z^3 =$

12) $15xy \times 2x^3y =$

13) $14pq^4 \times (-3p^3q) =$

14) $25s^4t^2 \times st^6 =$

15) $12p^5 \times (-2p^3) =$

16) $(-12p^2q^4r) \times 3pq^5r^3 =$

17) $(-7a^4) \times (-4a^5b) =$

18) $4u^7v^2 \times (-9u^4v^6) =$

19) $9u^5 \times (-3u) =$

20) $-3xy^9 \times 8x^5y =$

21) $12y^5z^3 \times (-2y^2z) =$

22) $9a^3bc^5 \times 4abc^3 =$

23) $(-9p^5q^2) \times (-3p^2q^4) =$

24) $4u^8v^3 \times (-4u^8v^5) =$

25) $15y^3z^4 \times (-y^5z) =$

26) $(-12pq^4r^3) \times 5p^4q^2r =$

27) $3ab^5c^2 \times 3a^2bc^4 =$

28) $7x^5yz^3 \times 9x^5y^7z^4 =$

Multiplying and Dividing Monomials

✎ **Simplify each expression.**

1) $(7x^2)(x^3) =$

2) $(4x^3)(5x^2) =$

3) $(3x^4)(2x^2) =$

4) $(5x^8)(8x^3) =$

5) $(12x^6)(2x^3) =$

6) $(2yx^5)(16x^2) =$

7) $(9x^5y)(2x^2y^3) =$

8) $(-2x^2y^5)(5x^3y^2) =$

9) $(-4x^2y^2)(-8x^4y^3) =$

10) $(2x^4y)(-5x^5y^3) =$

11) $(9x^4y^4)(2x^3y^3) =$

12) $(2x^4y^6)(3x^4y^3) =$

13) $(8x^3y^8)(7x^5y^{10}) =$

14) $(14x^6y^5)(3x^5y^5) =$

15) $(8x^2y^8)(5x^{10}y^{10}) =$

16) $(-3x^2y^5)(4x^6y^3) =$

17) $\dfrac{9x^4y^5}{xy^3} =$

18) $\dfrac{18x^8y^3}{18x^7y} =$

19) $\dfrac{54x^4y^4}{6xy} =$

20) $\dfrac{63x^4y^5}{7x^3y^4} =$

21) $\dfrac{32x^7y^6}{8x^2y^3} =$

22) $\dfrac{63x^9y^4}{3x^4y^3} =$

23) $\dfrac{96x^{16}y^{12}}{12x^7y^9} =$

24) $\dfrac{60x^{10}y^6}{12x^{11}y^3} =$

25) $\dfrac{90x^8y^{12}}{18x^7y^{12}} =$

26) $\dfrac{45x^{23}y^{10}}{9x^9y^6} =$

27) $\dfrac{-96x^8y^8}{24x^6y^8} =$

Multiplying a Polynomial and a Monomial

✎ **Find each product.**

1) $2x(x + 4) =$

2) $3(8 - x) =$

3) $5x(3x + 4) =$

4) $x(-2x + 5) =$

5) $7x(3x - 3) =$

6) $3(2x - 5y) =$

7) $6x(7x - 3) =$

8) $x(12x + 5y) =$

9) $5x(x + 6y) =$

10) $11x(4x + 5y) =$

11) $8x(4x + 2) =$

12) $12x(x - 15y) =$

13) $9x(5x - 3y) =$

14) $8x(5x - 2y + 5) =$

15) $9x(2x^2 + 7y^2) =$

16) $8x(9x + 6y) =$

17) $2(3x^5 - 2y^5) =$

18) $4x(-x^2y + 2y) =$

19) $-3(2x^3 - 3xy + 9) =$

20) $2(x^2 - 2xy - 4) =$

21) $7x(4x^3 - xy + 2x) =$

22) $-9x(-2x^3 - 2x + 7xy) =$

23) $6(x^2 + 3xy - 8y^2) =$

24) $5x(7x^3 - x + 8) =$

25) $7(x^{24} - 4x - 6) =$

26) $x^2(-3x^3 + 4x + 7) =$

27) $x^2(2x^3 + 10 - 5x) =$

28) $4x^4(3x^3 - 2x + 8) =$

29) $5x^2(x^4 - 5xy + 2y^3) =$

30) $4x^2(7x^4 - 2x + 11) =$

31) $7x^3(3x^3 + 5x - 7) =$

32) $4x(x^2 - 8xy + 7y^3) =$

Multiplying Binomials

✎ **Find each product.**

1) $(x + 5)(x + 1) =$

2) $(x - 3)(x + 7) =$

3) $(x - 1)(x - 9) =$

4) $(x + 3)(x + 8) =$

5) $(x - 4)(x - 11) =$

6) $(x + 5)(x + 6) =$

7) $(x - 8)(x + 7) =$

8) $(x - 3)(x - 2) =$

9) $(x + 8)(x + 11) =$

10) $(x - 3)(x + 5) =$

11) $(x + 8)(x + 8) =$

12) $(x + 2)(x + 7) =$

13) $(x - 9)(x + 4) =$

14) $(x - 10)(x + 10) =$

15) $(x + 24)(x + 2) =$

16) $(x + 9)(x + 13) =$

17) $(x - 7)(x + 7) =$

18) $(x - 5)(x + 2) =$

19) $(3x + 4)(x + 5) =$

20) $(x - 8)(5x + 2) =$

21) $(x - 9)(4x + 9) =$

22) $(2x - 7)(3x - 2) =$

23) $(x - 4)(x + 11) =$

24) $(5x - 6)(2x + 4) =$

25) $(4x - 9)(x + 7) =$

26) $(8x - 5)(2x + 2) =$

27) $(3x + 9)(7x + 4) =$

28) $(6x - 8)(4x + 4) =$

29) $(4x + 5)(5x - 8) =$

30) $(8x - 1)(8x + 4) =$

31) $(9x + 4)(3x - 6) =$

32) $(4x^2 + 12)(4x^2 - 12) =$

Factoring Trinomials

✎ **Factor each trinomial.**

1) $x^2 + 12x + 35 =$

2) $x^2 - 8x + 12 =$

3) $x^2 + 11x + 10 =$

4) $x^2 - 12x + 27 =$

5) $x^2 - 16x + 15 =$

6) $x^2 - 13x + 40 =$

7) $x^2 + 15x + 44 =$

8) $x^2 + x - 72 =$

9) $x^2 - 81 =$

10) $x^2 - 17x + 70 =$

11) $x^2 + 8x - 48 =$

12) $x^2 + 5x - 104 =$

13) $x^2 - 7x - 18 =$

14) $x^2 + 22x + 121 =$

15) $3x^2 - 3x - 36 =$

16) $2x^2 - 35x + 75 =$

17) $14x^2 + 11x - 15 =$

18) $8x^2 - 12x - 20 =$

19) $15x^2 + 16x + 4 =$

20) $24x^2 + 2x - 1 =$

✎ **Calculate each problem.**

21) The area of a rectangle is $x^2 - 3x - 40$. If the width of rectangle is $x - 8$, what is its length? _____

22) The area of a parallelogram is $12x^2 + 7x - 10$ and its height is $4x + 5$. What is the base of the parallelogram? _____

23) The area of a rectangle is $10x^2 - 43x + 28$. If the width of the rectangle is $5x - 4$, what is its length? _____

Operations with Polynomials

✎ Find each product.

1) $2(4x + 1) =$ _____

2) $5(2x + 7) =$ _____

3) $4(6x - 5) =$ _____

4) $-4(7x - 8) =$ _____

5) $3x^2(8x + 4) =$ _____

6) $6x^2(2x - 9) =$ _____

7) $5x^3(-x + 4) =$ _____

8) $-5x^4(4x - 9) =$ _____

9) $6(x^2 + 7x - 3) =$ _____

10) $4(3x^2 - 2x + 6) =$ _____

11) $9(3x^2 + 8x + 2) =$ _____

12) $7x(x^2 + 5x + 3) =$ _____

13) $(7x + 2)(2x - 5) =$ _____

14) $(8x + 5)(3x - 8) =$ _____

15) $(4x + 2)(6x - 1) =$ _____

16) $(5x - 4)(5x + 9) =$ _____

✎ Calculate each problem.

17) The measures of two sides of a triangle are $(2x + 8y)$ and $(5x - 3y)$. If the perimeter of the triangle is $(11x + 6y)$, what is the measure of the third side? _____

18) The height of a triangle is $(8x + 2)$ and its base is $(2x - 6)$. What is the area of the triangle? _____

19) One side of a square is $(4x + 3)$. What is the area of the square? _____

20) The length of a rectangle is $(7x - 9y)$ and its width is $(13x + 9y)$. What is the perimeter of the rectangle? _____

21) The side of a cube measures $(x + 2)$. What is the volume of the cube? _____

22) If the perimeter of a rectangle is $(24x + 10y)$ and its width is $(4x + 3y)$, what is the length of the rectangle? _____

Answers of Worksheets – Chapter 8

Writing Polynomials in Standard Form

1) $2x$

2) -6

3) $-11x^3 + 3x^2$

4) $19x^4 + 4$

5) $-4x^5 + 3x^2 + 9x$

6) $12x^7 - 7x^3$

7) $-2x^6 + 6x^2 + 9x$

8) $-9x^4 - 5x^3 + x$

9) $8x^2 - 21x + 34$

10) $11x^4 - 7x + 8$

11) $-13x^4 + 25x^3 + 45x$

12) $-2x^3 + 9x^2 + 17$

13) $8x^3 + 18x^2 - 8x$

14) $-10x^5 - 9x^4 - 4x^2$

15) $-8x^4 + 7x^2 - 41$

16) $-7x^5 + 3x^3 + 8x^2 - 12$

17) $-9x^5 - 8x^4 + 4x^2 + 12$

18) $-2x^5 - 9x^2 - x$

19) $6x^5 + 7x^4 - 8x^2$

20) $3x^8 - 15x^4 + 11x^2$

21) $-16x^5 + 17x^4 - 9x^2$

22) $-3x^5 + 37x^3 + 5x^2$

23) $-18x^3 + 6x^2 + 15x$

24) $12x^7 + 24x^4$

25) $6x^3 + 48x^2 + 24x$

26) $32x^4 - 16x^2 + 24x$

27) $14x^4 - 14x^3 + 14x$

28) $25x^6 + 20x^5 - 5x$

29) $52x^5 + 4x^4 + 2x^2$

30) $-24x^5 + 42x^3 + 18x^2$

Simplifying Polynomials

1) $3x - 36$

2) $10x^2 - 20x$

3) $35x^2 - 7x$

4) $18x^2 + 12x$

5) $10x^2 - 35x$

6) $9x^2 + 72x$

7) $3x^2 - 17x + 24$

8) $3x^2 - 23x - 36$

9) $x^2 - 13x + 40$

10) $9x^2 - 16$

11) $25x^2 - 50x + 16$

12) $-6x^4 + 14x^2$

13) $7x^3 - 2x^2 + 5x + 10$

14) $-5x^3 + 2x^2 + 8x$

15) $4x^5 - 8x^2 + 15x$

16) $7x^5 + 11x^4 - 4x^2$

17) $-2x^4 + 8x^3 - 14x^2 + 5x$

18) $-10x^3 + x^2 + 31$

19) $2x^3 + x^2 - 4x$

20) $-9x^3 - 4x^2 + 15$

21) $-2x^5 + 2x^4 - 18x^2$

22) $4x^3 - 5$

23) $-12x^5 - 12x^3$

24) -80

25) $-9x^3 + 2x^2 - 2x + 14$

26) $-4x^3 - 2x^2 + 14$

27) $12x^2 - 7x + 5$

28) $4x^4 - 11x^3 - 5x^2$

29) $6x^2 + 4x - 8$

30) $14x^4 - 5x^2 + 5$

31) $-8x^5 - 36$

32) $10x^3 - 2x$

Adding and Subtracting Polynomials

1) $3x^2 - 1$

2) $4x^2 - 2$

3) $-4x^3 + 4x^2 - 15$

4) $3x^3 - x$

5) $-4x^3 + 14x - 7$

6) $8x^2$

7) $14x^3 - 6$

8) $x^2 - 5$

9) $4x^2 + 4x$

10) $15x$

11) $15x^4 - 5x$

12) $-8x^4 - 5x$

13) $-10x^5 + 7x^3 + 2x$

14) $5x^5 + 5x^3 - 7$

15) $4x^4 + 15x^2$

16) $-12x^2 + 3x$

17) $-21x^4 - x$

18) $-5x^4 + 3x^3 + 4x$

19) $13x^3 - 6x^2 - 7$

20) $14x^5 + 6x^4$

21) $15x^4 + 22x^3 + 8x^2$

22) $9x^2 - 10x$

23) $56x^3 + 5x$

24) $2x^5 - 11x^3 - 2x^2 - 3x$

25) $8x^5 + 18x^3 - 10x$

26) $29x^4 + 11x^3 + 2x^2$

Multiplying Monomials

1) $-7u^7$

2) $36p^{10}$

3) $20xy^3z^5$

4) $16u^7t^3$

5) $10a^5b^3$

6) $-20a^6b^3$

7) $20x^3y^6$

8) $-8p^3q^6$

9) $24s^6t^8$

10) $-49x^9y^4$

11) $15xy^7z^4$

12) $30x^4y^2$

13) $-42p^4q^5$

14) $25s^5t^8$

15) $-24p^8$

16) $-36p^3q^9r^4$

17) $28a^9b$

18) $-36u^{11}v^8$

19) $-27u^6$

20) $-24x^6y^{10}$

21) $-24y^7z^4$

22) $36a^4b^2c^8$

23) $27p^7q^6$

24) $-16u^{16}v^8$

25) $-15y^8z^5$

26) $-60p^5q^6r^4$

27) $9a^3b^6c^6$

28) $63x^{10}y^8z^7$

Multiplying and Dividing Monomials

1) $7x^5$

2) $20x^5$

3) $6x^6$

4) $40x^{11}$

5) $24x^9$

6) $32x^7y$

7) $18x^7y^4$

8) $-10x^5y^7$

9) $32x^6y^5$

10) $-10x^9y^4$

11) $18x^7y^7$

12) $6x^8y^9$

13) $56x^8y^{18}$

14) $42x^{11}y^{10}$

15) $40x^{12}y^{18}$

16) $-12x^8y^8$

17) $9x^3y^2$

18) xy^2

19) $9x^3y^3$

20) $9xy$

21) $4x^5y^3$

22) $21x^5y$

23) $8x^9y^3$

24) $5x^{-1}y^3$

25) $5x$

26) $5x^{14}y^4$

27) $-4x^2$

Multiplying a Polynomial and a Monomial

1) $2x^2 + 8x$

2) $-3x + 24$

3) $15x^2 + 20x$

4) $-2x^2 + 5x$

5) $21x^2 - 21x$

6) $6x - 15y$

7) $42x^2 - 18x$

8) $12x^2 + 5xy$

9) $5x^2 + 30xy$

10) $44x^2 + 55xy$

11) $32x^2 + 16x$

12) $12 - 180xy$

13) $45x^2 - 27xy$

14) $40x^2 - 16xy + 40x$

15) $18x^3 + 63xy^2$

16) $72x^2 + 48xy$

17) $6x^5 - 2y^5$

18) $-4x^3y + 8xy$

19) $-6x^3 + 9xy - 27$

20) $2x^2 - 4xy - 8$

21) $28x^4 - 7x^2y + 14x^2$

22) $18x^4 + 18x^2 - 63x^2y$

23) $6x^2 + 18xy - 48y^2$

24) $35x^4 - 5x^2 + 40x$

25) $7x^{24} - 28x - 42$

26) $-3x^5 + 4x^3 + 7x^2$

27) $2x^5 - 5x^3 + 10x^2$

28) $12x^7 - 8x^5 + 32x^4$

29) $5x^6 - 25x^3y + 10x^2y^3$

30) $28x^6 - 8x^3 + 44x^2$

31) $21x^6 + 35x^4 - 49x^3$

32) $4x^3 - 32x^2y + 28xy^3$

Multiplying Binomials

1) $x^2 + 6x + 5$

2) $x^2 + 4x - 21$

3) $x^2 - 10x + 9$

4) $x^2 + 11x + 24$

5) $x^2 - 15x + 44$

6) $x^2 + 11x + 30$

7) $x^2 - x - 56$

8) $x^2 - 5x + 6$

9) $x^2 + 19x + 88$

10) $x^2 + 2x + 15$

11) $x^2 + 16x + 64$

12) $x^2 + 9x + 14$

13) $x^2 - 5x - 36$

14) $x^2 - 100$

15) $x^2 + 26x + 48$

16) $x^2 + 22x + 117$

17) $x^2 - 49$

18) $x^2 - 3x - 10$

19) $3x^2 + 19x + 20$

20) $5x^2 - 38x - 16$

21) $4x^2 - 27x - 81$

22) $6x^2 - 25x + 14$

23) $x^2 + 7x - 44$

24) $10x^2 + 8x - 24$

25) $4x^2 + 19x - 63$

26) $16x^2 + 6x - 10$

27) $21x^2 + 75x + 36$

28) $24x^2 - 8x - 32$

29) $20x^2 - 7x - 40$

30) $64x^2 + 24x - 4$

31) $27x^2 - 42x - 24$

32) $16x^4 - 144$

Factoring Trinomials

1) $(x + 5)(x + 7)$

2) $(x - 2)(x - 6)$

3) $(x + 1)(x + 10)$

4) $(x - 9)(x - 3)$

5) $(x - 1)(x - 15)$

6) $(x - 5)(x - 8)$

7) $(x + 4)(x + 11)$

8) $(x + 9)(x - 8)$

9) $(x - 9)(x + 9)$

10) $(x - 7)(x - 10)$

11) $(x - 4)(x + 12)$

12) $(x - 8)(x + 13)$

13) $(x + 2)(x - 9)$

14) $(x + 11)(x + 11)$

15) $(3x + 9)(x - 4)$

16) $(x - 15)(2x - 5)$

17) $(7x - 5)(2x + 3)$

18) $(2x - 5)(4x + 4)$

19) $(3x + 2)(5x + 2)$

20) $(6x - 1)(4x + 1)$

21) $(x + 5)$

22) $(3x - 2)$

23) $(2x - 7)$

Operations with Polynomials

1) $8x + 2$

2) $10x + 35$

3) $24x - 20$

4) $-28x + 32$

5) $24x^3 + 12x^2$

6) $12x^3 - 54x^2$

7) $-5x^4 + 20x^3$

8) $-20x^5 + 45x^4$

9) $6x^2 + 42x - 18$

10) $12x^2 - 8x + 24$

11) $27x^2 + 72x + 18$

12) $7x^3 + 35x^2 + 21x$

13) $14x^2 - 31x - 10$

14) $24x^2 - 49x - 40$

15) $24x^2 + 8x - 2$

16) $25x^2 + 25x - 36$

17) $(4x + y)$

18) $8x^2 - 22x - 6$

19) $16x^2 + 24x + 9$

20) $40x$

21) $x^3 + 6x^2 + 12x + 8$

22) $(8x + 2y)$

Chapter 9: Functions Operations and Quadratic

Topics that you will practice in this chapter:

- ✓ Graphing Quadratic Functions
- ✓ Solving Quadratic Equations
- ✓ Use the Quadratic Formula and the Discriminant
- ✓ Solve Quadratic Inequalities
- ✓ Evaluating Function
- ✓ Adding and Subtracting Functions
- ✓ Multiplying and Dividing Functions
- ✓ Composition of Functions

It's fine to work on any problem, so long as it generates interesting mathematics along the way – even if you don't solve it at the end of the day." – Andrew Wiles

Evaluating Function

✎ Write each of following in function notation.

1) $h = -8x + 9$

2) $k = 5a - 21$

3) $d = 14t$

4) $y = \frac{3}{17}x - \frac{9}{17}$

5) $m = 18n - 94$

6) $c = p^2 - 7p + 15$

✎ Evaluate each function.

7) $f(x) = 6x - 7$, find $f(-3)$

8) $g(x) = \frac{1}{10}x + 6$, find $f(5)$

9) $h(x) = -2x + 15$, find $f(8)$

10) $f(x) = -3x + 8$, find $f(-2)$

11) $f(a) = 12a - 9$, find $f(0)$

12) $h(x) = 18 - 5x$, find $f(-4)$

13) $g(n) = 7n - 5$, find $f(5)$

14) $f(x) = -9x - 2$, find $f(3)$

15) $k(n) = -12 + 4.5n$, find $f(2)$

16) $f(x) = -1.5x + 2.5$, find $f(-6)$

17) $g(n) = \frac{16n-8}{6n}$, find $g(2)$

18) $g(n) = \sqrt{5n} - 2$, find $g(5)$

19) $h(x) = x^{-1} - 6$, find $h(\frac{1}{9})$

20) $h(n) = n^{-3} + 4$, find $h(\frac{1}{2})$

21) $h(n) = n^2 - 5$, find $h(\frac{4}{5})$

22) $h(n) = n^3 - 8$, find $h(-\frac{1}{3})$

23) $h(n) = 4n^2 - 42$, find $h(-4)$

24) $h(n) = -5n^2 - 9n$, find $h(7)$

25) $g(n) = \sqrt{4n^2} - \sqrt{5n}$, find $g(5)$

26) $h(a) = \frac{-15a+7}{3a}$, find $h(-b)$

27) $k(a) = 8a - 9$, find $k(a - 3)$

28) $h(x) = \frac{1}{6}x + 7$, find $h(-12x)$

29) $h(x) = 8x^2 + 10$, find $h(\frac{x}{2})$

30) $h(x) = x^4 - 8$, find $h(-2x)$

Adding and Subtracting Functions

✎ **Perform the indicated operation.**

1) $f(x) = 2x + 3$

   $g(x) = x + 4$

   Find $(f - g)(2)$

2) $g(a) = -3a - 8$

   $f(a) = -4a - 12$

   Find $(g - f)(-2)$

3) $h(t) = 7t + 5$

   $g(t) = 3t + 11$

   Find $(h - g)(t)$

4) $g(a) = -5a - 3$

   $f(a) = 3a^2 + 4$

   Find $(g - f)(x)$

5) $g(x) = \frac{2}{7}x - 10$

   $h(x) = \frac{5}{7}x + 10$

   Find $g(14) - h(14)$

6) $h(3) = \sqrt{7x} - 2$

   $g(x) = \sqrt{7x} + 2$

   Find $(h + g)(7)$

7) $f(x) = x^{-3}$

   $g(x) = x^2 + \frac{4}{x}$

   Find $(f - g)(-1)$

8) $h(n) = n^2 + 8$

   $g(n) = -n + 5$

   Find $(h - g)(a)$

9) $g(x) = -2x^2 - 3 - x$

   $f(x) = 7 + x$

   Find $(g - f)(2x)$

10) $g(t) = 4t - 9$

    $f(t) = -t^2 + 5$

    Find $(g + f)(-z)$

11) $f(x) = 3x + 9$

    $g(x) = -4x^2 + 2x$

    Find $(f - g)(-x^2)$

12) $f(x) = -9x^3 - 4x$

    $g(x) = 4x + 12$

    Find $(f + g)(3x^2)$

Multiplying and Dividing Functions

✎ **Perform the indicated operation.**

1) $g(x) = -2x - 5$

$f(x) = 3x + 4$

Find $(g.f)(2)$

2) $f(x) = 3x$

$h(x) = -2x + 5$

Find $(f.h)(-3)$

3) $g(a) = 5a - 3$

$h(a) = a - 7$

Find $(g.h)(-3)$

4) $f(x) = x - 4$

$h(x) = 4x - 3$

Find $(\frac{f}{h})(4)$

5) $f(x) = 9a^2$

$g(x) = 5 + 4a$

Find $(\frac{f}{g})(3)$

6) $g(a) = \sqrt{5a} + 7$

$f(a) = (-a)^2 + 3$

Find $(\frac{g}{f})(5)$

7) $g(t) = t^2 + 5$

$h(t) = 2t - 5$

Find $(g.h)(-3)$

8) $g(n) = n^2 + 2n - 4$

$h(n) = -n + 6$

Find $(g.h)(1)$

9) $g(a) = (a - 7)^3$

$f(a) = a^2 + 8$

Find $(\frac{g}{f})(7)$

10) $g(x) = -x^2 + \frac{4}{5}x + 10$

$f(x) = x^2 - 3$

Find $(\frac{g}{f})(5)$

11) $f(x) = x^3 - 3x^2 + 9$

$g(x) = x - 4$

Find $(f.g)(x)$

12) $f(x) = 3x - 5$

$g(x) = x^2 - 4x$

Find $(f.g)(x^2)$

Composition of Functions

✎ Using $f(x) = 2x - 5$ and $g(x) = -2x$, find:

1) $f(g(0)) =$

4) $g(f(3)) =$

2) $f(g(-1)) =$

5) $f(g(-2)) =$

3) $g(f(1)) =$

6) $g(f(5)) =$

✎ Using $f(x) = -\frac{1}{4}x + \frac{3}{4}$ and $g(x) = x^2$, find:

7) $g(f(4)) =$

10) $f(f(1)) =$

8) $g(f(3)) =$

11) $g(f(-1)) =$

9) $g(g(2)) =$

12) $g(f(7)) =$

✎ Using $f(x) = -5x + 2$ and $g(x) = x + 3$, find:

13) $g(f(0)) =$

16) $f(g(-3)) =$

14) $f(f(2)) =$

17) $g(f(-5)) =$

15) $f(g(3)) =$

18) $f(f(x)) =$

✎ Using $f(x) = \sqrt{x + 9}$ and $g(x) = x - 9$, find:

19) $f(g(9)) =$

22) $f(f(-5)) =$

20) $g(f(-8)) =$

23) $g(f(7)) =$

21) $f(g(18)) =$

24) $g(g(8)) =$

Quadratic Equation

✎ Multiply.

1) $(x - 2)(x + 8) = $ _____

2) $(x + 1)(x + 9) = $ _____

3) $(x - 5)(x + 6) = $ _____

4) $(x + 7)(x - 3) = $ _____

5) $(x - 9)(x - 8) = $ _____

6) $(4x + 2)(x - 4) = $ _____

7) $(3x - 6)(x + 4) = $ _____

8) $(x - 9)(2x + 7) = $ _____

9) $(5x + 3)(x - 4) = $ _____

10) $(4x + 2)(3x - 3) = $ _____

✎ Factor each expression.

11) $x^2 - 4x - 21 = $ _____

12) $x^2 + 14x + 45 = $ _____

13) $x^2 - 5x - 24 = $ _____

14) $x^2 - 7x + 6 = $ _____

15) $x^2 + 14x + 33 = $ _____

16) $4x^2 + 38x + 18 = $ _____

17) $5x^2 + 18x - 8 = $ _____

18) $2x^2 + 2x - 40 = $ _____

19) $2x^2 + 22x + 56 = $ _____

20) $12x^2 - 148x + 360 = $ _____

✎ Calculate each equation.

21) $(x + 6)(x - 9) = 0$

22) $(x + 1)(x + 11) = 0$

23) $(3x + 9)(x + 3) = 0$

24) $(5x - 5)(6x + 12) = 0$

25) $x^2 - 12x + 30 = 6$

26) $x^2 + 6x + 14 = 5$

27) $x^2 + \frac{9}{2}x + 7 = 5$

28) $x^2 + 2x - 25 = 10$

29) $2x^2 + 12x - 54 = 0$

30) $x^2 - 11x = 12$

Solving Quadratic Equations

✍ **Solve each equation by factoring or using the quadratic formula.**

1) $(x + 5)(x - 2) = 0$

2) $(x + 8)(x + 2) = 0$

3) $(x - 9)(x + 5) = 0$

4) $(x - 3)(x - 1) = 0$

5) $(x + 9)(x + 4) = 0$

6) $(2x + 5)(x + 9) = 0$

7) $(9x + 8)(3x + 9) = 0$

8) $(4x + 2)(x + 5) = 0$

9) $(x + 2)(2x + 9) = 0$

10) $(12x + 3)(2x + 9) = 0$

11) $2x^2 = 16x$

12) $x^2 - 16 = 0$

13) $2x^2 + 48 = 22x$

14) $-x^2 - 20 = 9x$

15) $x^2 + 8x = 33$

16) $2x^2 + 12x = 80$

17) $x^2 + 14x = -48$

18) $x^2 + 15x = -54$

19) $x^2 + 15x = -36$

20) $x^2 + 2x - 40 = 5x$

21) $x^2 + 16x = -63$

22) $x^2 - 18x = -81$

23) $10x^2 = 7x - 1$

24) $7x^2 - 5x + 8 = 8$

25) $8x^2 + 27 = 33x$

26) $5x^2 - 26x = -24$

27) $3x^2 + 6 = -19x$

28) $x^2 + 22x = -117$

29) $x^2 + 3x - 58 = 30$

30) $5x^2 + 20x - 200 = 25$

31) $3x^2 - 33x + 84 = 0$

32) $6x^2 - 31x + 30 = 15 - 10x^2$

Graphing Quadratic Functions

✎ **Sketch the graph of each function. Identify the vertex and axis of symmetry.**

1) $y = (x + 3)^2 + 5$

2) $y = (x - 3)^2 - 1$

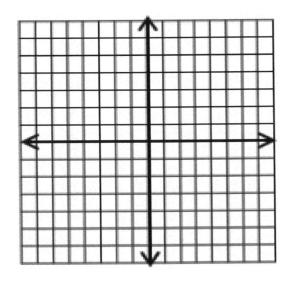
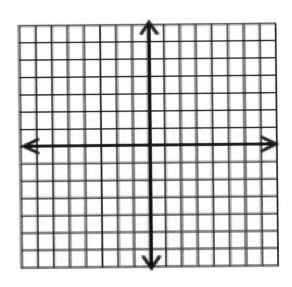

3) $y = 6 - (-x + 2)^2$

4) $y = -3x^2 - 6x + 9$

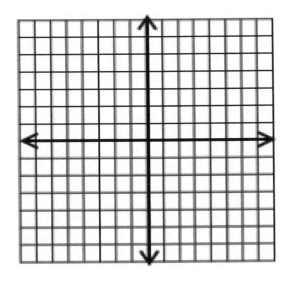
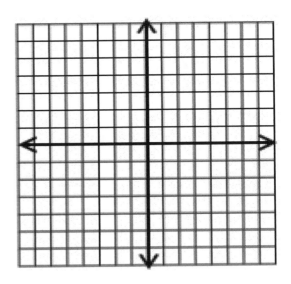

Answers of Worksheets – Chapter 9

Evaluating Function

1) $h(x) = -8x + 9$

2) $k(a) = 5a - 21$

3) $d(t) = 14t$

4) $y(x) = \frac{3}{17}x - \frac{9}{17}$

5) $m(n) = 18n - 94$

6) $c(p) = p^2 - 7p + 15$

7) -25

8) 6.5

9) -1

10) 14

11) -9

12) 38

13) 30

14) -29

15) -3

16) 11.5

17) 2

18) 3

19) 3

20) 12

21) $-\frac{109}{25}$

22) $-\frac{215}{27}$

23) 22

24) -308

25) 5

26) $-\frac{15b+7}{3b}$

27) $8a - 33$

28) $-2x + 7$

29) $2x^2 + 10$

30) $-16x^4 - 8$

Adding and Subtracting Functions

1) 1

2) 2

3) $4t - 6$

4) $-3x^2 - 5x - 7$

5) -26

6) 14

7) 2

8) $a^2 + a + 3$

9) $-8x^2 - 4x - 10$

10) $-z^2 - 4z - 4$

11) $4x^4 - x^2 + 9$

12) $-243x^6 + 12$

Multiplying and Dividing Functions

1) -90

2) -99

3) 180

4) 0

5) $\frac{81}{17}$

6) $\frac{3}{7}$

7) -154

8) -5

9) 0

10) $-\frac{1}{2}$

11) $x^4 - 7x^3 + 12x^2 + 9x - 36$

12) $3x^6 - 17x^4 + 20x^2$

Composition of Functions

1) -5

2) -1

3) 6

4) -2

5) 3

6) -10

7) $\frac{1}{16}$

8) 0

9) 16

10) $\frac{5}{8}$

11) 1

12) 1

13) 5

14) 42

15) -28

16) 2

17) 30

18) $25x - 8$

19) 3

20) -8

21) $3\sqrt{2}$

22) $\sqrt{11}$

23) -5

24) -10

Quadratic Equations

1) $x^2 + 6x - 16$

2) $x^2 + 10x + 9$

3) $x^2 + x - 30$

4) $x^2 + 4x - 21$

5) $x^2 - 17x + 72$

6) $4x^2 - 14x - 8$

7) $3x^2 + 6x - 24$

8) $2x^2 - 11x - 63$

9) $5x^2 - 17x - 12$

10) $12x^2 - 6x - 6$

11) $(x - 7)(x + 3)$

12) $(x + 5)(x + 9)$

13) $(x - 8)(x + 3)$

14) $(x - 1)(x - 6)$

15) $(x + 3)(x + 11)$

16) $(4x + 2)(x + 9)$

17) $(5x - 2)(x + 4)$

18) $(2x - 8)(x + 5)$

19) $(2x + 8)(x + 7)$

20) $4(x - 9)(3x - 10)$

21) $x = -6, x = 9$

22) $x = -1, x = -11$

23) $x = -3$

24) $x = 1, x = -2$

25) $x = 6$

26) $x = -3$

27) $x = -4, x = -\frac{1}{2}$

28) $x = 5, x = -7$

29) $x = 3, x = -9$

30) $x = -1, x = 12$

Solving quadratic equations

1) $\{-5, 2\}$

2) $\{-8, -2\}$

3) $\{9, -5\}$

4) $\{3, 1\}$

5) $\{-9, -4\}$

6) $\{-\frac{5}{2}, -9\}$

7) $\{-\frac{8}{9}, -3\}$

8) $\{-\frac{1}{2}, -5\}$

9) $\{-2, -\frac{9}{2}\}$

10) $\{-\frac{1}{4}, -\frac{9}{2}\}$

11) $\{8, 0\}$

12) $\{4, -4\}$

13) $\{3, 8\}$

14) $\{-5, -4\}$

15) $\{3, -11\}$

16) $\{4, -10\}$

17) $\{-6, -8\}$

18) $\{-6, -9\}$

19) $\{-3, -12\}$

20) $\{8, -5\}$

21) $\{-7, -9\}$

22) $\{9\}$

23) $\{\frac{1}{5}, \frac{1}{2}\}$

24) $\{\frac{5}{7}, 0\}$

25) $\{\frac{9}{8}, 3\}$

26) $\{\frac{6}{5}, 4\}$

27) $\{-\frac{1}{3}, -6\}$

28) $\{-9, -13\}$

29) $\{8, -11\}$

30) $\{5, -9\}$

31) $\{4, 7\}$

32) $\{\frac{15}{16}, 1\}$

Graphing quadratic functions

1) $(-3, 5), x = -3$

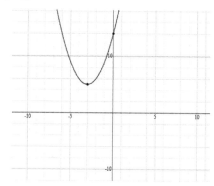

2) $(3, -1), x = 3$

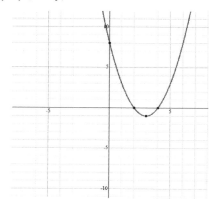

3) $(2, 6), x = 2$

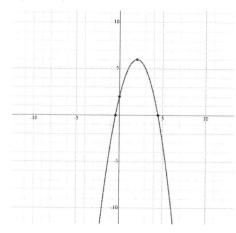

1) $(-1, 12), x = -1$

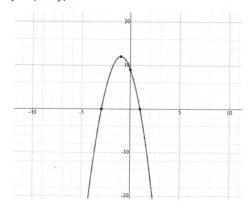

Chapter 10:

Geometry and Solid Figures

Topics that you will practice in this chapter:

- ✓ Angles
- ✓ Pythagorean Relationship
- ✓ Triangles
- ✓ Polygons
- ✓ Trapezoids
- ✓ Circles
- ✓ Cubes
- ✓ Rectangular Prism
- ✓ Cylinder
- ✓ Pyramids and Cone

Mathematics is, as it were, a sensuous logic, and relates to philosophy as do the arts, music, and plastic art to poetry. — *K. Shegel*

Angles

✎ **What is the value of x in the following figures?**

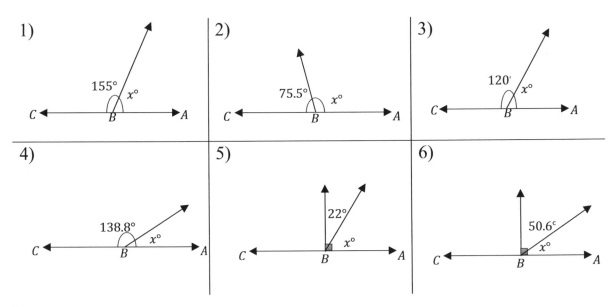

✎ **Calculate**.

7) Two supplementary angles have equal measures. What is the measure of each angle? _____

8) The measure of an angle is nine seventh the measure of its supplement. What is the measure of the angle? _____

9) Two angles are complementary and the measure of one angle is 24 less than the other. What is the measure of the bigger angle? _____

10) Two angles are complementary. The measure of one angle is one fifth the measure of the other. What is the measure of the smaller angle? _____

11) Two supplementary angles are given. The measure of one angle is 80° less than the measure of the other. What does the bigger angle measure? _____

Pythagorean Relationship

✍ Do the following lengths form a right triangle?

1)

8   11   7

2)
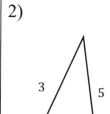
3   5   4

3)
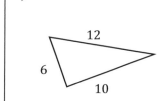
12   6   10

4)
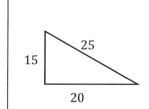
25   15   20

5)
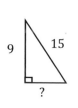
32   40   24

6)
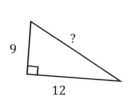
16   8   12

7)
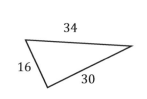
26   24   10

8)
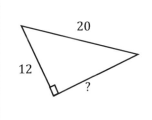
34   16   30

✍ Find the missing side?

9)
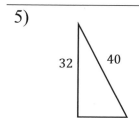
9   ?   12

10)
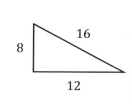
24   ?   18

11)
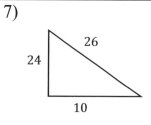
?   24   45

12)
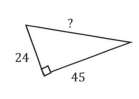
13   12   ?

13)
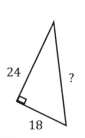
9   15   ?

14)
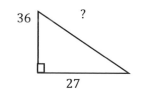
36   ?   27

15)
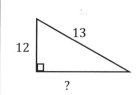
30   18   ?

16)

20   12   ?

Triangles

✎ **Find the measure of the unknown angle in each triangle.**

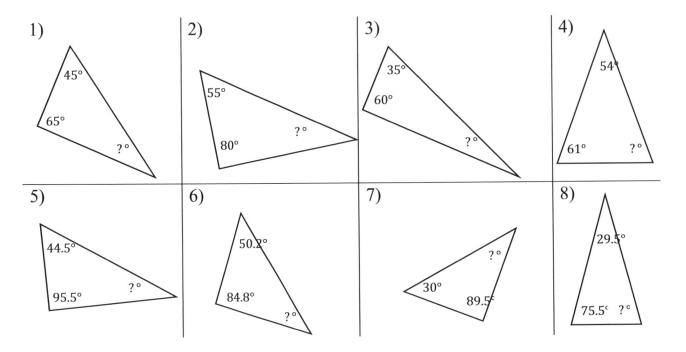

1)

45°
65°
?°

2)

55°
80°
?°

3)

35°
60°
?°

4)

54°
61°
?°

5)

44.5°
95.5°
?°

6)

50.2°
84.8°
?°

7)

?°
30°
89.5°

8)

29.5°
75.5°
?°

✎ **Find area of each triangle.**

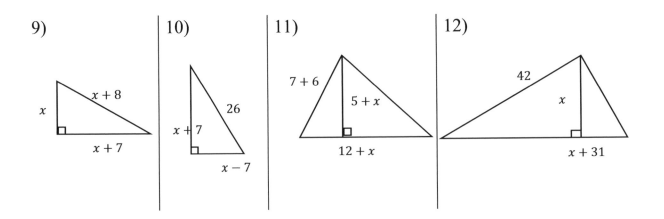

9)

x
$x + 8$
$x + 7$

10)

$x + 7$
26
$x - 7$

11)

$7 + 6$
$5 + x$
$12 + x$

12)

42
x
$x + 31$

Polygons

✎ Find the perimeter of each shape.

1)

x ft

x ft x ft

x ft

2)

x +2

x in x in

x+2

3)

1-y ft   1-y ft

1-y ft   1-y ft

4) Square

$(x + 1)$ cm

5) Regular hexagon

$(2x)$ m

6)

$(x - 0.5)$ cm $(x + 1.5)$ cm

x cm

$(x + 1.5)$ cm $(x - 0.5)$ cm

7) Parallelogram

$(x + 1)$ in

$(x + 3)$ in

8) Square

$(x + 2)$ m

✎ Find the area of each shape.

9) Parallelogram

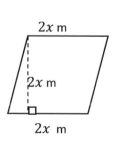

2x m

2x m

2x m

10) Rectangle

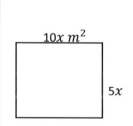

10$x\ m^2$

5x

11) Rectangle

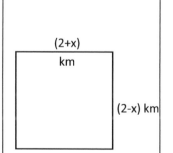

(2+x) km

(2-x) km

12) Square

0.6x m

Trapezoids

✍ **Find the area of each trapezoid.**

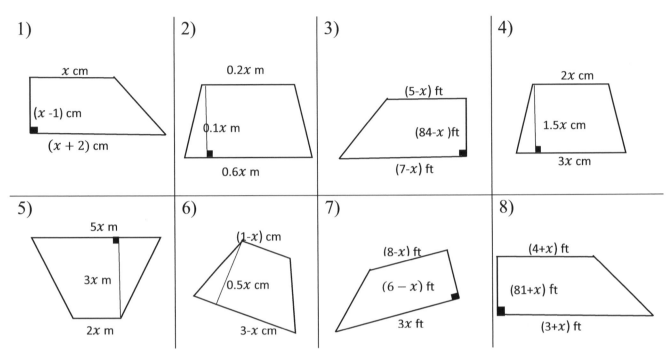

✍ **Calculate.**

1) A trapezoid has an area of 40 cm² and its height is 8 cm and one base is 6 cm. What is the other base length? _____

2) If a trapezoid has an area of 85 ft² and the lengths of the bases are 9 ft and 8 ft, find the height. _____

3) If a trapezoid has an area of 150 m² and its height is 15 m and one base is 9 m, find the other base length. _____

4) The area of a trapezoid is 196 ft² and its height is 14 ft. If one base of the trapezoid is 12 ft, what is the other base length?

_____

Circles

✍ **Find the area of each circle.** ($\pi = 3.14$)

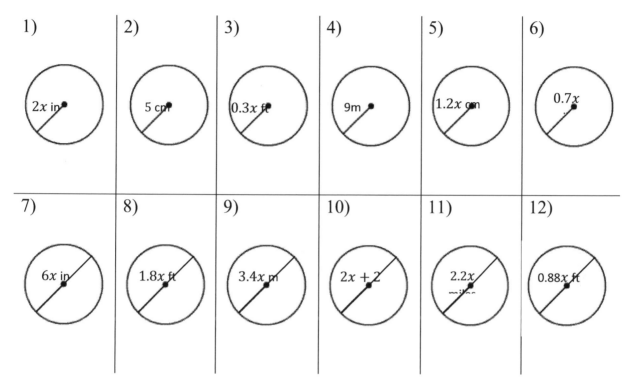

1) 2x in
2) 5 cm
3) 0.3x ft
4) 9m
5) 1.2x cm
6) 0.7x

7) 6x in
8) 1.8x ft
9) 3.4x m
10) 2x + 2
11) 2.2x miles
12) 0.88x ft

✍ **Complete the table below.** ($\pi = 3.14$)

Circle No.	Radius	Diameter	Circumference	Area
1	1.4 inches	2.8 inches	8.792 inches	6.154 square inches
2		4.6 meters		
3				$2.01x^2$ square ft
4			36.42 miles	
5		6.2x kilometers		
6	5x centimeters			
7		2x feet		
8				1.54 square meters
9			5.7x inches	
10	(1-x) feet			

Cubes

✏️ **Find the volume of each cube.**

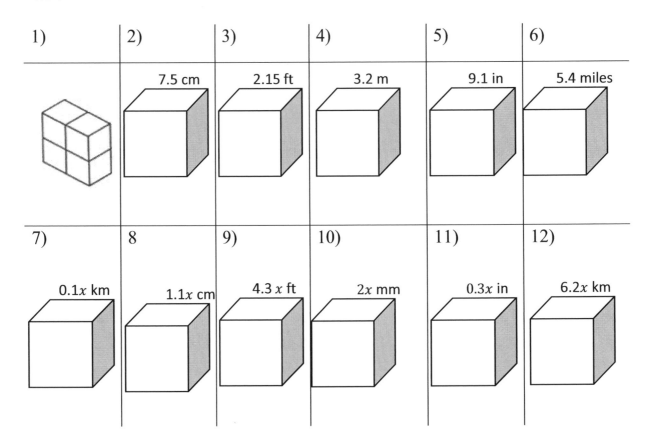

1)	2) 7.5 cm	3) 2.15 ft	4) 3.2 m	5) 9.1 in	6) 5.4 miles

7) 0.1x km	8) 1.1x cm	9) 4.3 x ft	10) 2x mm	11) 0.3x in	12) 6.2x km

✏️ **Find the surface area of each cube.**

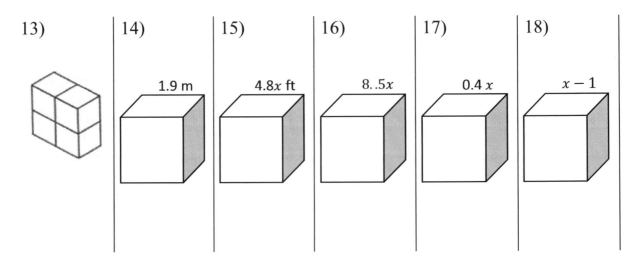

13)	14) 1.9 m	15) 4.8x ft	16) 8..5x	17) 0.4 x	18) $x-1$

Rectangular Prism

✒ **Find the volume of each Rectangular Prism.**

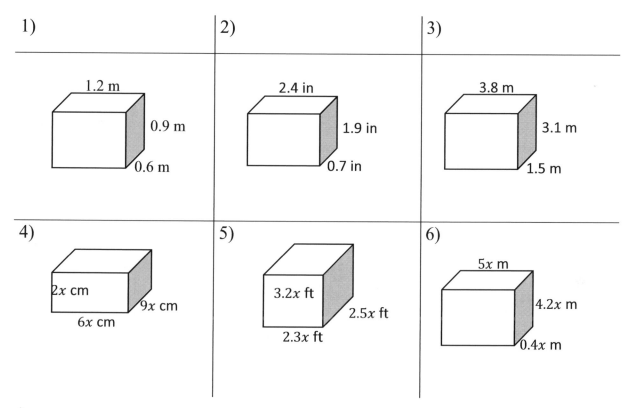

1)

1.2 m
0.9 m
0.6 m

2)

2.4 in
1.9 in
0.7 in

3)

3.8 m
3.1 m
1.5 m

4)

2x cm
9x cm
6x cm

5)

3.2x ft
2.5x ft
2.3x ft

6)

5x m
4.2x m
0.4x m

✒ **Find the surface area of each Rectangular Prism.**

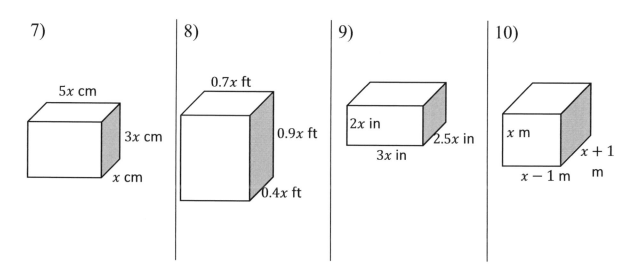

7)

5x cm
3x cm
x cm

8)

0.7x ft
0.9x ft
0.4x ft

9)

2x in
2.5x in
3x in

10)

x m
x + 1 m
x − 1 m

Cylinder

✎ **Find the volume of each Cylinder. Round your answer to the**

nearest tenth. ($\pi = 3.14$)

1)

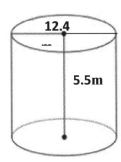

12.4

5.5m

2)

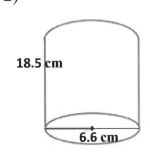

18.5 cm

6.6 cm

3)

12.8x

16.5 cm

4)

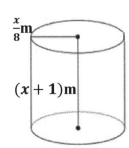

$\frac{x}{8}$m

$(x+1)$m

5)

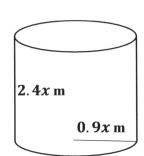

2.4x m

0.9x m

6)

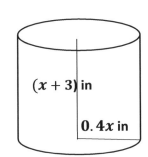

$(x+3)$ in

0.4x in

✎ **Find the surface area of each Cylinder.** ($\pi = 3.14$)

7)

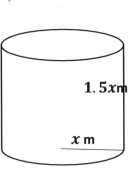

1.5xm

x m

8)

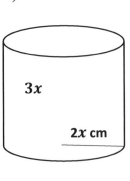

3x

2x cm

9)

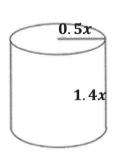

0.5x

1.4x

10)

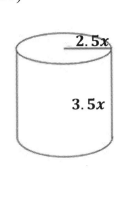

2.5x

3.5x

Pyramids and Cone

✎ **Find the volume of each Pyramid and Cone.** ($\pi = 3.14$)

1)

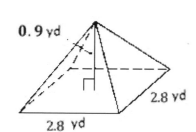

0.9 yd

2.8 yd

2.8 yd

2)

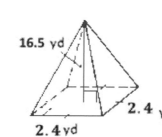

16.5 yd

2.4 yd

2.4 yd

3)

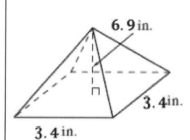

6.9 in.

3.4 in.

3.4 in.

4)

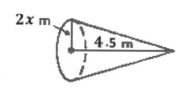

2x m

4.5 m

5)

14x m

6.5 m

6)

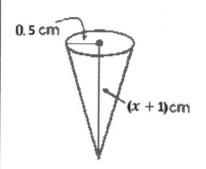

0.5 cm

(x + 1)cm

✎ **Find the surface area of each Pyramid and Cone.** ($\pi = 3.14$)

7)

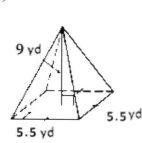

9 yd

5.5 yd

5.5 yd

8)

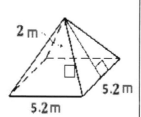

2 m

5.2 m

5.2 m

9)

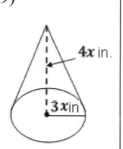

4x in.

3x in

10)

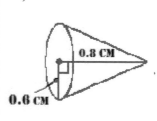

0.8 CM

0.6 CM

Answers of Worksheets – Chapter 10

Angles

1) $25°$
2) $104.5°$
3) $60°$
4) $41.2°$
5) $68°$
6) $39.4°$
7) $90°$
8) $101.25°$
9) $57°$
10) $15°$
11) $130°$

Pythagorean Relationship

1) *No*
2) *Yes*
3) *No*
4) *Yes*
5) *Yes*
6) *No*
7) *Yes*
8) *Yes*
9) 15
10) 30
11) 51
12) 5
13) 12
14) 45
15) 24
16) 16

Triangles

1) $70°$
2) $45°$
3) $85°$
4) $65°$
5) $40°$
6) $45°$
7) $60.5°$
8) $75°$
9) $(\frac{x^2+7x}{2})$ square unites
10) $(\frac{x^2-49}{2})$ square unites
11) $(\frac{x^2+17x+60}{2})$ square unites
12) $(\frac{x^2+31x}{2})$ *square unites*

Polygons

1) $(4x)\ ft$
2) $(4x + 4)\ in$
3) $(4 - 4y)\ ft$
4) $(4x + 4)\ cm$
5) $(12x)\ m$
6) $(4x + 2)\ cm$
7) $(4x + 8)\ in$
8) $(4x + 8)\ m$
9) $(4x^2)m^2$
10) $(50x^2)m^2$
11) $(4 - x^2)\ km^2$
12) $(0.36x^2)\ m^2$

Trapezoids

1) $(x^2 - 1)\ cm^2$
2) $(0.04x^2)\ m^2$
3) $(x^2 - 10x + 24)\ ft^2$
4) $(3.75x^2)\ cm^2$
5) $(10.5x^2)m^2$
6) $(x - 0.5x^2)cm^2$
7) $(-x^2 + 2x + 24)\ ft^2$
8) $(\frac{2x^2+9x+7}{2})ft^2$

Calculate

1) 4 cm
2) 10 ft
3) 11 m
4) 16 ft

Circles

1) $(12.56x^2)\ in^2$
2) $78.5\ cm^2$
3) $(0.283x^2)\ ft^2$
4) $254.34m^2$
5) $(4.522x^2)cm^2$
6) $(1.54x^2)\ miles^2$
7) $(28.56x^2)\ in^2$
8) $(2.543x^2)ft^2$
9) $(9.075x^2)\ m^2$

10) $(3.14x^2 + 6.28x + 3.14)\ cm^2$ 11) $(3.8x^2)\ miles^2$ 12) $(0.608x^2)\ ft^2$

Circle No.	Radius	Diameter	Circumference	Area
1	1.4 inches	2.8 inches	8.792 inches	6.154 square inches
2	2.3 meters	4.6 meters	14.44 meters	16.61 meters
3	$0.8x$ square ft	$1.6x$ square ft	$5.024x$ square ft	$2.01x^2$ square ft
4	5.8 miles	11.6 miles	36.42 miles	105.63 miles
5	$3.1x$ kilometers	$6.2x$ kilometers	$19.47x$ kilometers	$30.175x^2$ kilometers
6	$5x$ centimeters	$10x$ centimeters	$31.4x$ centimeters	$78.5x^2$ centimeters
7	x feet	$2x$ feet	$6.28x$ feet	$3.14x^2$ feet
8	0.7 square meters	1.4 square meters	4.396 square meters	1.54 square meters
9	$2.5x$ inches	$5x$ inches	$15.7x$ inches	$19.625x^2$ inches
10	$(1-x)$ feet	$2 - 2x$ feet	$6.28 - 6.28x)$ feet	$3.14x^2 - 6.28x + 3.14)$ feet

Cubes

1) 4
2) $421.88\ cm^3$
3) $9.94\ ft^3$
4) $32.77\ m^3$
5) $753.57\ in^3$

6) $157.46\ miles^3$
7) $(0.001x^3)\ km^3$
8) $(1.33x^3)\ cm^3$
9) $(79.51x^3)\ ft^3$
10) $(8x^3)\ mm^3$

11) $(0.027x^3)\ in^3$
12) $(238.33x^3)\ km^3$
13) 12
14) $21.66\ m^2$
15) $(138.24x^2)\ ft^2$

16) $(433.5x^2)\ mm^2$
17) $(0.96x^2)\ km^2$
18) $6x^2 - 12x + 6\ cm^2$

Rectangular Prism

1) $0.65\ m^3$
2) $3.19\ in^3$
3) $17.67\ m^3$

4) $(108x^3)\ cm^3$
5) $(18.4x^3)\ ft^3$
6) $(8.4x^3)\ m^3$

7) $(46x^2)\ cm^2$
8) $(2.54x^2)\ ft^2$
9) $(37x^2)\ in^2$

10) $(6x^2 - 2)\ m^2$

Cylinder

1) $663.86\ m^3$
2) $632.6\ cm^3$
3) $(8,488.55x^2)\ cm^3$

4) $(0.05x^3 + 0.05x^2)\ m^3$
5) $(6.104x^3)\ m^3$

6) $(0.5\ x^3 + 1.51x^2)in^3$
7) $(15.7x^2)\ m^2$

8) $(62.8x^2)\ cm^2$
9) $(5.97x^2)\ cm^2$
10) $(94.2x^2)\ m^2$

Pyramids and Cone

1) $2.35\ yd^3$
2) $31.68\ yd^3$
3) $26.59\ in^3$

4) $(18.84x^2)\ m^3$
5) $(619.10x)\ m^3$
6) $(0.262x +$

0.262) cm^3
7) $133.77yd^2$
8) $61.15\ m^2$

9) $(75.36x^2)in^2$
10) $(3.01)cm^2$

Chapter 11:
Statistics and Probability

Topics that you will practice in this chapter:

- ✓ Mean and Median
- ✓ Mode and Range
- ✓ Histograms
- ✓ Stem–and–Leaf Plot
- ✓ Pie Graph
- ✓ Probability Problems
- ✓ Factorials
- ✓ Combinations and Permutation

Mathematics is no more computation than typing is literature.

– John Allen Paulos

Mean and Median

✍ Find Mean and Median of the Given Data.

1) 8, 9, 19, 3, 4

2) 11, 7, 35, 10, 17, 32, 24

3) 38, 9, 15, 17, 13

4) 50, 19, 2, 18, 6, 7

5) 25, 27, 13, 16, 6, 13, 54

6) 24, 364, 42, 57, 6, 68

7) 89, 98, 65, 45, 3, 4, 30, 42

8) 34, 15, 15, 17, 22, 29, 15

9) 2, 5, 10, 45, 8, 13, 35, 6

10) 20, 22, 18, 7, 2, 17, 44, 53

11) 33, 52, 81, 9, 45, 31

12) 19, 74, 51, 8, 12, 15, 9, 14

✍ Calculate.

13) In a javelin throw competition, five athletics score 45, 33, 53, 46 and 19 meters. What are their Mean and Median? _____

14) Eva went to shop and bought 5 apples, 9 peaches, 4 bananas, 7 pineapples and 8 melons. What are the Mean and Median of her purchase? _____

15) Bob has 19 black pen, 15 red pen, 27 green pens, 21 blue pens and one boxes of yellow pens. If the Mean and Median are 19 respectively, what is the number of yellow pens in box? _____

Mode and Range

✍ Find Mode and Rage of the Given Data.

1) 7, 4, 18, 9, 9, 3

    Mode: _____   Range: _____

2) 8, 8, 15, 14, 8, 5, 6, 18

    Mode: _____   Range: _____

3) 4, 4, 4, 15, 19, 24, 31, 5, 4

    Mode: _____   Range: _____

4) 10, 10, 9, 17, 14, 8, 20, 4

    Mode: _____   Range: _____

5) 5, 11, 3, 4, 3, 3

    Mode: _____   Range: _____

6) 13, 7, 7, 7, 7, 4, 12, 25, 8, 3

    Mode: _____   Range: _____

7) 1, 7, 9, 9, 24, 24, 24, 20, 34, 35

    Mode: _____   Range: _____

8) 9, 4, 7, 13, 13, 13, 9, 8, 15

    Mode: _____   Range: _____

9) 8, 8, 8, 5, 8, 7, 17, 16, 3, 9

    Mode: _____   Range: _____

10) 34, 34, 32, 14, 6, 14, 9, 14

    Mode: _____   Range: _____

11) 8, 8, 6, 8, 18, 10, 16, 15

    Mode: _____   Range: _____

12) 12, 12, 7, 11, 14, 12, 33, 5

    Mode: _____   Range: _____

✍ Calculate.

13) A stationery sold 21 pencils, 42 red pens, 25 blue pens, 26 notebooks, 21 erasers, 28 rulers and 27 color pencils. What are the Mode and Range for the stationery sells?

          Mode: _____   Range: _____

14) In an English test, eight students score 19, 10, 10, 17, 35, 35, 14 and 10. What are their Mode and Range? _____

15) What is the range of the first 6 odd numbers greater than 8?

    _____

Times Series

✍ Use the following Graph to complete the table.

Day	Distance (km)
1	
2	

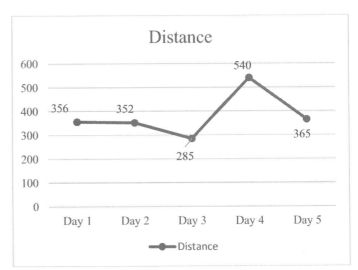

The following table shows the number of births in the US from 2007 to 2012 (in millions).

Year	Number of births (in millions)
2007	4.25
2008	4.19
2009	4.55
2010	3.80
2011	3.25
2012	2.54

Draw a Time Series for the table.

Stem–and–Leaf Plot

✑ **Make stem ad leaf plots for the given data.**

1) 41, 44, 47, 40, 70, 45, 79, 77, 49, 44, 19, 10

Stem	Leaf plot

2) 21, 87, 56, 20, 27, 23, 55, 82, 82, 53, 87, 58

Stem	Leaf plot

3) 111, 47, 66, 44, 94, 117, 62, 114, 48, 112, 68, 99

Stem	Leaf plot

4) 52, 25, 101, 58, 71, 26, 109, 53, 75, 29, 53, 108, 79

Stem	Leaf plot

5) 51, 88, 9, 87, 81, 8, 3, 50, 85, 54, 9, 54, 5

Stem	Leaf plot

6) 40, 93, 20, 25, 48, 92, 95, 52, 21, 44, 97, 29

Stem	Leaf plot

Pie Graph

The circle graph below shows all Robert's expenses for last month. Robert spent $384 on his hobbies last month.

Answer following questions based on the Pie graph.

1) How much was Robert's total expenses last month? _____

2) How much did Robert spend on his car last month? _____

3) How much did Robert spend for shopping last month? _____

4) How much did Robert spend on his rent last month? _____

5) What fraction is Robert's expenses for his car and shopping out of his total expenses last month? _____

Probability Problems

✎ Calculate.

1) A number is chosen at random from 1 to 20. Find the probability of selecting number 8 or smaller numbers. _____

2) Bag A contains 16 red marbles and 6 green marbles. Bag B contains 12 black marbles and 18 orange marbles. What is the probability of selecting a green marble at random from bag A? What is the probability of selecting a black marble at random from Bag B? _____

3) A number is chosen at random from 1 to 25. What is the probability of selecting multiples of 5? _____

4) A card is chosen from a well-shuffled deck of 52 cards. What is the probability that the card will be a queen? _____

5) A number is chosen at random from 1 to 15. What is the probability of selecting a multiple of 4? _____

A spinner numbered 1–8, is spun once. What is the probability of spinning …?

6) an Odd number? _____

7) a multiple of 2? _____

8) a multiple of 5? _____

9) number 10? _____

Factorials

✎ **Determine the value for each expression.**

1) $6! + 1! =$

2) $5! + 2! =$

3) $(4!)^2 =$

4) $6! - 3! =$

5) $8! - 4! + 3 =$

6) $3! \times 4 - 12 =$

7) $(3! + 1!)^2 =$

8) $(5! - 4!)^2 =$

9) $(3! \, 0!)^2 - 2 =$

10) $\dfrac{8!}{6!} =$

11) $\dfrac{3!}{2!} =$

12) $\dfrac{6!}{5!} =$

13) $\dfrac{21!}{19!} =$

14) $\dfrac{(n-1)!}{(n-3)!} =$

15) $\dfrac{(n+2)!}{(n+1)!} =$

16) $\dfrac{(4+2!)^3}{2!} =$

17) $\dfrac{4n!}{2n!} =$

18) $\dfrac{31!}{29!2!} =$

19) $\dfrac{13!}{9!3!} =$

20) $\dfrac{6 \times 280!}{3(4 \times 70)!} =$

21) $\dfrac{30!}{31!2!} =$

22) $\dfrac{7!7!}{8!5!} =$

23) $\dfrac{12!11!}{9!10!} =$

24) $\dfrac{(2 \times 5)!}{1!9!} =$

25) $\dfrac{2!(6n-1)!}{(6n)!} =$

26) $\dfrac{n(4n+4)!}{(4n+5)!} =$

27) $\dfrac{(n+1)!(n)}{(n+2)!} =$

Combinations and Permutations

✎ **Calculate the value of each.**

1) $6! = $ ____

2) $2! \times 5! = $ ____

3) $4! = $ ____

4) $3! + 5! = $ ____

5) $7! = $ ____

6) $9! = $ ____

7) $3! + 3! = $ ____

8) $5! - 2! = $ ____

✎ **Find the answer for each word problems.**

9) Susan is baking cookies. She uses sugar, Vanilla and eggs. How many different orders of ingredients can she try? _____

10) Albert is planning for his vacation. He wants to go to museum, watch a movie, go to the beach, play volleyball and play football. How many ways of ordering are there for him? _____

11) How many 6-digit numbers can be named using the digits 1, 6, 8, 9, and 10 without repetition? _____

12) In how many ways can 4 boys be arranged in a straight line? _____

13) In how many ways can 8 athletes be arranged in a straight line? _____

14) A professor is going to arrange her 5 students in a straight line. In how many ways can she do this? _____

15) How many code symbols can be formed with the letters for the word FRIEND? _____

16) In how many ways a team of 7 basketball players can choose a captain and co-captain? _____

Answers of Worksheets – Chapter 11

Mean and Median

1) Mean: 8.6, Median: 8
2) Mean: 19.43, Median: 17
3) Mean: 18.4, Median: 15
4) Mean: 17, Median: 12.5
5) Mean: 22, Median: 16

6) Mean: 93.5, Median: 49.5
7) Mean: 47, Median: 43.5
8) Mean: 21, Median: 17
9) Mean: 15.5, Median: 9
10) Mean: 22.88, Median: 19

11) Mean: 41.83, Median: 39
12) Mean: 25.25, Median: 14.5
13) Mean: 39.2, Median: 45
14) Mean: 6.6, Median: 7
15) 13

Mode and Range

1) Mode: 9, Range: 15
2) Mode: 8, Range: 13
3) Mode: 4, Range: 27
4) Mode: 10, Range: 16
5) Mode: 3, Range: 8

6) Mode: 7, Range: 22
7) Mode: 24, Range: 34
8) Mode: 13, Range: 11
9) Mode: 8, Range: 14
10) Mode: 14, Range: 28

11) Mode: 8, Range: 12
12) Mode: 12, Range: 28
13) Mode: 21, Range: 21
14) Mode: 10, Range: 25
15) 10

Time series

Day	Distance (km)
1	356
2	352
3	285
4	540
5	365

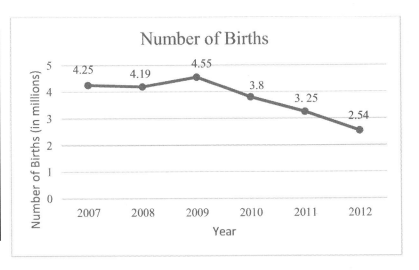

Stem–And–Leaf Plot

1)

Stem	leaf
1	0 9
4	0 1 4 4 5 7 9
7	0 7 9

2)

Stem	leaf
2	0 1 3 7
5	3 5 6 8
8	2 2 7 7

3)

Stem	leaf
4	4 7 8
6	2 6 8
9	4 9
11	1 2 4 7

4)

Stem	leaf
2	5 6 9
5	2 3 3 8
7	1 5 9
10	1 8 9

5)

Stem	leaf
0	3 5 8 9 9
5	0 1 4 4
8	1 5 7 8

6)

Stem	leaf
2	0 1 5 9
4	0 2 4 8
9	2 3 5 7

Pie Graph

1) $1,600

2) $232

3) $312

4) $520

5) $\frac{17}{50}$

Probability Problems

1) $\frac{2}{5}$

2) $\frac{3}{11}, \frac{2}{5}$

3) $\frac{1}{5}$

4) $\frac{1}{13}$

5) $\frac{1}{5}$

6) $\frac{1}{2}$

7) $\frac{1}{2}$

8) $\frac{1}{8}$

9) 0

Factorials

1) 721

2) 122

3) 576

4) 714

5) 40,299

6) 12

7) 49

8) 9,216

9) 34

10) 56

11) 3

12) 6

13) 420

14) $(n-1)(n-2)$

15) $n+2$

16) 108

17) 2

18) 465

19) 2,860

20) 2

21) $\frac{1}{62}$

22) 5.25

23) 14,520

24) 10

25) $\frac{1}{3n}$

26) $\frac{n}{4n+5}$

27) $\frac{n}{n+2}$

Combinations and Permutations

1) 720

2) 240

3) 24

4) 126

5) 5,040

6) 362,880

7) 12

8) 118

9) 6

10) 120

11) 720

12) 24

13) 40,320

14) 120

15) 720

16) 42

ASVAB Math Practice Tests

The Armed Services Vocational Aptitude Battery (ASVAB) was introduced in 1968. Over 40 million examinees have taken the ASVAB since then.

According to official ASVAB website, the ASVAB is a multiple-aptitude battery that measures developed abilities and helps predict future academic and occupational success in the military. It is administered annually to more than one million military applicants, high school, and post-secondary students.

ASVAB scores are reported as percentiles between 1-99. An ASVAB percentile score indicates the percentage of examinees in a reference group that scored at or below that score. For example, ASVAB score of 90 indicates that the examinee scored as well as or better than 90% of the nationally representative sample test takers. An ASVAB score of 60 indicates that the examinee scored as well as or better than 60% of the nationally representative sample.

There are three types of ASVAB:

- The CAT-ASVAB (computer adaptive test)
- The MET-site ASVAB (paper and pencil (P&P)
- The Student ASVAB (paper and pencil (P&P)

The CAT-ASVAB is a computer adaptive test. It means that if the correct answer is chosen, the next question will be harder. If the answer given is incorrect, the next question will be easier. This also means that once an answer is selected on the CAT it cannot be changed.

The MET- site ASVAB and The Student ASVAB are paper and pencil (P&P) tests.

In this section, there are 10 complete Arithmetic Reasoning and Mathematics Knowledge ASVAB Tests. There are 5 complete tests for CAT-ASVAB and 5 complete tests for paper and pencil (P&P).

Take these tests to see what score you'll be able to receive on a real ASVAB test.

Good luck!

ASVAB practice Test 1 - CAT

Arithmetic Reasoning

○ **16 questions**

○ **Total time for this section:** 39 Minutes

○ **Calculators are not allowed for this test.**

Administered *Month Year*

1) Mia is 8 years older than her sister Elise, and Elise is 5 years younger than her brother Mason. If the sum of their ages is 61, how old is Elise?

   A. 16   C. 19

   B. 20   D. 15

2) John is driving to visit his mother, who lives 540 miles away. How long will the drive be, round–trip, if John drives at an average speed of 18 mph?

   A. 60 Minutes   C. 7,200 Minutes

   B. 1,200 Minutes   D. 3,600 Minutes

3) While at work, Emma checks her email once every 70 minutes. In 7–hour, how many times does she check her email?

   A. 5 Times   C. 7 Times

   B. 10 Times   D. 6 Times

4) Julie gives 9 pieces of candy to each of her friends. If Julie gives all her candy away, which amount of candy could have been the amount she distributed?

   A. 168   C. 856

   B. 738   D. 472

5) If a rectangle is 30 feet by 48 feet, what is its area?

   A. 2,880   C. 480

   B. 1,440   D. 720

6) You are asked to chart the temperature during a 6-hour period to give the average. These are your results:

6 am: 4 degrees   3 pm: 30 degrees

2 am: 6 degrees   11 pm: 22 degrees

10 am: 21 degrees   1 pm: 31 degrees

What is the average temperature?

A. 22   C. 19

B. 18   D. 20

7) Each year, a cybercafé charges its customers a base rate of $18, with an additional $0.35 per visit for the first 40 visits, and $0.3 for every visit after that. How much does the cybercafé charge a customer for a year in which 50 visits are made?

A. $30   C. $45

B. $20   D. $35

8) If a vehicle is driven 53 miles on Monday, 57 miles on Tuesday, and 40 miles on Wednesday, what is the average number of miles driven each day?

A. 50 Miles   C. 39 Miles

B. 43 Miles   D. 45 Miles

9) What is the prime factorization of 360?

A. $2 \times 3 \times 3 \times 5$ C. 3×7

B. $2 \times 2 \times 2 \times 3 \times 3 \times 5$ D. $2 \times 3 \times 3 \times 7$

10) Three co-workers contributed $18.47, $28.25, and $31.12 respectively to purchase a retirement gift for their boss. What is the maximum amount they can spend on a gift?

A. 3730.4

B. $77.84

C. $57.45

D. $87.48

11) A family owns 21 dozen of magazines. After donating 76 magazines to the public library, how many magazines are still with the family?

A. 96

B. 186

C. 176

D. 626

12) In the deck of cards, there are 8 spades, 7 hearts, 14 clubs, and 19 diamonds. What is the probability that William will pick out a spade?

A. $\frac{1}{3}$

B. $\frac{1}{6}$

C. $\frac{1}{5}$

D. $\frac{1}{9}$

13) William is driving a truck that can hold 9 tons maximum. He has a shipment of food weighing 54,000 pounds. How many trips will he need to make to deliver all the food?

A. 2 Trip

B. 3 Trips

C. 18 Trips

D. 6 Trips

14) A man goes to a casino with $220. He loses $60 on blackjack, then loses another $90 on roulette. How much money does he have left?

    A. $20   C. $70

    B. $80   D. $110

15) A woman owns a dog walking business. If 3 workers can walk 9 dogs, how many dogs can 4 workers walk?

    A. 16   C. 3

    B. 9   D. 12

16) Aria was hired to teach six identical math courses, which entailed being present in the classroom 36 hours altogether. At $25 per class hour, how much did Aria earn for teaching one course?

    A. $360   C. $160

    B. $250   D. $150

ASVAB practice Test 1 - CAT

Mathematics Knowledge

- o **Total time for this section: 18 Minutes**

- o **16 questions**

- o **Calculators are not allowed for this test.**

Administered *Month Year*

1) Which of the following is not equal to 7^2?

A. the square of 7

C. 7 cubed

B. 7 squared

D. 7 to the second power

2) If a = 9, what is the value of b in this equation? $b = \frac{a^2}{3} + 2$

A. 20

C. 27

B. 18

D. 29

3) The sixth root of 64 is:

A. 3

C. 2

B. 6

D. 5

4) A circle has a radius of 5 inches. What is its approximate area? ($\pi = 3.14$)

A. 7.85 square inches

C. 85.7 square inches

B. 78.5 square inches

D. 75 square inches

5) If $-7a = 63$, then $a =$ ___

A. -9

C. 8

B. 9

D. 7

6) In the following diagram what is the value of x?

A. 43

B. 28

C. 142

D. 38

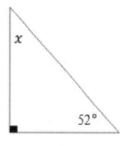

7) What is 826,470 in scientific notation?

A. 82.647

C. 0.082647×10^6

B. 8.2647×10^5

D. 0.82647

8) In the following right triangle, what is the value of x rounded to the nearest hundredth?

A. 12

B. 5

C. 10

D. 9

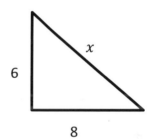

9) $(2x + 2)(4x + 3) = ?$

A. $8x^2 + 6$

C. $8x^2 + 14x + 6$

B. $8x^2 + 10x + 3$

D. $8x^2 + 10$

10) $6(a - 3) = 18$, what is the value of a?

A. 36

C. 6.6

B. 3

D. 6

11) If $9^{12} = 3^9 \times 3^{3x}$, what is the value of x?

    A. 12   C. 8

    B. 4   D. 5

12) Which of the following is an obtuse angle?

    A. 152°   C. 68°

    B. 60°   D. 35°

13) Factor this expression: $x^2 - 6x + 8$

    A. $x^2(4x - 2)$ C. $(x - 4)(x - 2)$

    B. $2x(x + 4)$ D. $(x + 4)(x - 2)$

14) Find the slope of the line running through the points $(1, 4)$ and $(3, 8)$.

    A. $\dfrac{1}{3}$ C. 3

    B. 2   D. $-\dfrac{1}{3}$

15) What is the value of $\sqrt{144} \times \sqrt{36}$?

    A. 48   C. 72

    B. $\sqrt{169}$ D. $\sqrt{242}$

16) The cube root of 343 is?

    A. 16   C. 7.5

    B. 7   D. 10

ASVAB practice Test 2
Paper and Pencil

ASVAB Arithmetic Reasoning

- **Total time for this section:** 36 Minutes

- **30 questions**

- **Calculators are not allowed for this test.**

Administered *Month Year*

1) Camille uses a 40% off coupon when buying a sweater that costs $60. If she also pays 8% sales tax on the purchase, how much does she pay?

A. $28.8   C. $48.28

B. $36.8   D. $38.88

2) Will has been working on a report for 2 hours each day, 6 days a week for 4 weeks. How many minutes has Will worked on his report?

A. 24   C. 148

B. 2,880   D. 4,760

3) James is driving to visit his mother, who lives 240 miles away. How long will the drive be, round–trip, if James drives at an average speed of 40 mph?

A. 480 minutes   C. 1,440 minutes

B. 720 minutes   D. 1,260 minutes

4) In a classroom of 80 students, 28 are female. What percentage of the class is male?

A. 36%   C. 52%

B. 65%   D. 45%

5) Which of the following is NOT a factor of 24?

A. 12   C. 8

B. 6   D. 14

6) You are asked to chart the temperature during a 6-hour period to give the average. These are your results:

2 am: 6 degrees   12 am: 22 degrees

5 am: 10 degrees   10 am: 18 degrees

6 am: 25 degrees   11 pm: 21 degrees

What is the average temperature?

A. 16   C. 17

B. 16.5   D. 19.5

7) During the last week of track training, Emma achieves the following times in seconds: 51, 54, 37, 43, 51, and 46. Her three best times this week (least times) are averaged for her final score on the course. What is her final score?

A. 42 seconds   C. 46 seconds

B. 54 seconds   D. 43 seconds

8) How many square feet of tile is needed for 13 feet by 13 feet room?

A. 169 square feet   C. 240 square feet

B. 160 square feet   D. 60 square feet

9) With what number must 3.852369 be multiplied in order to obtain the number 385236.9?

A. 100   C. 1,000,000

B. 10,000   D. 100,000

10) Elsa is working in a hospital supply room and makes $20.00 an hour. The union negotiates a new contract giving each employee an 5% cost of living raise. What is Elsa's new hourly rate?

A. $25 an hour

C. $22 an hour

B. $5 an hour

D. $21 an hour

11) Emily and Lucas have taken the same number of photos on their school trip. Emily has taken 6 times as many photos as Mia. Lucas has taken 30 more photos than Mia. How many photos has Mia taken?

A. 6

C. 30

B. 12

D. 35

12) Which answer is equivalent to three to the sixth power?

A. 0.0007

C. 0.729

B. 72,900

D. 729

13) Find the average of the following numbers: 20, 31, 27, 42, 25

A. 28

C. 29

B. 29.5

D. 28.3

14) A mobile classroom is a rectangular block that is 51 feet by 43 feet in length and width respectively. If a student walks around the block once, how many yards does the student cover?

A. 1,880 yards

C. 188 yards

B. 94 yards

D.148yards

15) What is the distance in miles of a trip that takes 3.4 hours at an average speed of 23.5 miles per hour? (Round your answer to a whole number)

    A. 78 miles

    B. 80 miles

    C. 89 miles

    D. 69 miles

16) The sum of 7 numbers is greater than 150 and less than 200. Which of the following could be the average (arithmetic mean) of the numbers?

    A. 15

    B. 25

    C. 18

    D. 38

17) A barista averages making 19 coffees per hour. At this rate, how many hours will it take until she's made 1,900 coffees?

    A. 55 hours

    B. 60 hours

    C. 100 hours

    D. 110 hours

18) Nicole was making $6.30 per hour and got a raise to $6.68 per hour. What percentage increase was Nicole's raise?

    A. 38%

    B. 60.3%

    C. 6.03%

    D. 3.80%

19) An architect's floor plan uses $\frac{1}{4}$ inch to represent one mile. What is the actual distance represented by $4\frac{1}{4}$ inches?

    A. 17 miles

    B. 18 miles

    C. 7 miles

    D. 8 miles

20) A snack machine accepts only quarters. Candy bars cost 70¢, a package of peanuts costs 50¢, and a can of cola costs 30¢. How many quarters are needed to buy two Candy bars, one package of peanuts, and one can of cola?

A. 6 quarters

B. 9 quarters

C. 5 quarters

D. 4 quarters

21) A writer finishes 150 pages of his manuscript in 50 hours. How many pages is his average per hour?

A. 3

B. 6

C. 2

D. 1

22) I've got 42 quarts of milk and my family drinks 3 gallons of milk per week. How many weeks will that last us?

A. 5.25 weeks

B. 5.5 weeks

C. 3.5 weeks

D. 3.25 weeks

23) A floppy disk shows 752,135 bytes free and 635,086 bytes used. If you delete a file of size 867,234 bytes and create a new file of size 758,748 bytes, how many free bytes will the floppy disk have?

A. 680,261

B. 860,621

C. 860,821

D. 68,261

24) If $5y + 7y + 6y = -108$, then what is the value of y?

A. −5

B. −7

C. −6

D. 6

25) The hour hand of a watch rotates 30 degrees every hour. How many complete rotations does the hour hand make in 8 days?

    A. 16   C. 22

    B. 8   D. 38

26) What is the product of the square root of 64 and the square root of 25?

    A. 4.5   C. 30

    B. 40   D. 36

27) A bread recipe calls for $3\frac{4}{15}$ cups of flour. If you only have $2\frac{2}{5}$ cups of flour, how much more flour is needed?

    A. $2\frac{1}{5}$ C. $1\frac{2}{15}$

    B. $\frac{13}{15}$ D. $\frac{1}{5}$

28) There are 191 rooms that need to be painted and only 14 painters available. If there are still 23 rooms unpainted by the end of the day, what is the average number of rooms that each painter has painted?

    A. 15   C. 21

    B. 12   D. 11

29) Convert 0.092 to a percent.

    A. 0.9%   C. 9.20%

    B. 0.92%   D. 92%

30) If $8x - 11x + 3x = -27$, then what is the value of x?

A. Any Number

C. Negative Infinity

B. Does not exit

D. Positive Infinity

ASVAB practice Test 2
Paper and Pencil

ASVAB Mathematics Knowledge

- o **25 questions**

- o **Total time for this section:** 24 Minutes

- o **Calculators are not allowed for this test.**

Administered *Month Year*

1) Simplify: $5(3x^5)^3$.

   A. $135x^8$ C. $152x^{15}$

   B. $135x^{15}$ D. $135x^{25}$

2) What is the perimeter of the triangle in the provided diagram?

   A. 62

   B. 58

   C. 54

   D. 51

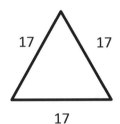

3) If x is a positive integer divisible by 6, and $x < 38$, what is the greatest possible value of x?

   A. 30 C. 36

   B. 16 D. 24

4) $(x + 8)(x + 2) =?$

   A. $x^2 - 10x + 10$ C. $x^2 + 10x + 10$

   B. $2x - 10x + 18$ D. $x^2 + 10x + 16$

5) Convert 820,000 to scientific notation.

   A. 8.2×10^5 C. 8.20×100

   B. 8.20×10^{-5} D. 8.20×1000

6) Which of the following is an obtuse angle?

   A. 45° C. 170°

   B. 185° D. 210°

7) $7^8 \times 7^7 =$?

    A. 7^{10} C. 7^{13}

    B. $7^{0.8}$ D. 7^{15}

8) What is 4,789.56126 rounded to the nearest tenth?

    A. 4,789.561   C. 4,789

    B. 4,789.6   D. 4,789.562

9) The cube root of 729 is?

    A. 9   C. 999

    B. 99   D. 81,811,999

10) A circle has a diameter of 16 inches. What is its approximate area? ($\pi = 3.14$)

    A. 160.96   C. 32.96

    B. 200.96   D. 116.96

11) There are two pizza ovens in a restaurant. Oven 1 burns six times as many pizzas as oven 2. If the restaurant had a total of 161 burnt pizzas on Saturday, how many pizzas did oven 2 burn?

    A. 17   C. 23

    B. 24   D. 27

12) Which of the following is the correct calculation for 7!?

    A. $210 \times 4!$ C. $3 \times 4 \times 5 \times 6!$

    B. $36 \times 6!$ D. $7 \times 8 \times 6!$

13) The equation of a line is given as: $y = 5x - 4$. Which of the following points does not lie on the line?

A. (2, 6)

C. (4, 16)

B. (−2, −10)

D. (−1, −9)

14) How long is the line segment shown on the number line below?

A. −9

C. 5

B. −4

D. 9

15) What is the distance between the points (4, 5) and (−1, −7)?

A. 15

C.10

B. 14

D. 13

16) $x^2 - 49 = 0$, x could be:

A. 7

C.6

B. 10

D. 11

17) A rectangular plot of land is measured to be 110 feet by 140 feet. Its total area is:

A. 15,400 square feet

C. 14,400 square feet

B.115,800square feet

D. 25,000 square feet

18) Which of the following is NOT a factor of 112?

  A. 56

  B. 7

  C. 28

  D. 9

19) The sum of 4 numbers is greater than 110 and less than 160. Which of the

  following could be the average (arithmetic mean) of the numbers?

  A. 45

  B. 60

  C. 38

  D. 52

20) One fifth the cube of 10 is:

  A. 50

  B. 20

  C. 200

  D. 2

21) What is the sum of the prime numbers in the following list of numbers?

  26, 13, 7, 16, 8, 23, 46, 52

  A. 29

  B. 19

  C. 34

  D. 43

22) Convert 30% to a fraction.

  A. $\frac{3}{20}$

  B. $\frac{1}{3}$

  C. $\frac{3}{10}$

  D. $\frac{3}{5}$

23) With what number must 8.54869 be multiplied in order to obtain the number

  8,548.69?

  A. 10

  B. 100

  C. 1,000

  D. 10,000

24) The supplement angle of a 65° angle is:

    A. 145°   C. 80°

    B. 115°   D. 25°

25) 25% of 80 is:

    A. 65   C. 20

    B. 55   D. 25

Answers and Explanations

ASVAB Practice Tests

Answer Key

✻ Now, it's time to review your results to see where you went wrong and what areas you need to improve!

ASVAB Math Practice Test

Test 1 CAT				Test 2 Paper and Pencil							
Arithmetic Reasoning		Mathematic Knowledge		Arithmetic				Mathematic Knowledge			
1	A	1	C	1	D	16	B	1	B	16	A
2	D	2	D	2	B	17	C	2	D	17	A
3	D	3	C	3	B	18	C	3	C	18	D
4	B	4	B	4	B	19	A	4	D	19	C
5	B	5	A	5	D	20	C	5	A	20	C
6	C	6	D	6	C	21	A	6	C	21	D
7	D	7	B	7	A	22	C	7	D	22	C
8	A	8	C	8	A	23	B	8	B	23	C
9	B	9	C	9	D	24	C	9	A	24	B
10	B	10	D	10	D	25	A	10	B	25	C
11	C	11	D	11	A	26	B	11	C		
12	B	12	A	12	D	27	B	12	A		
13	B	13	C	13	C	28	B	13	B		
14	C	14	B	14	C	29	C	14	D		
15	D	15	C	15	B	30	A	15	D		
16	D	16	B								

Answers and Explanations

Practice Test 1 - CAT

Arithmetic Reasoning

1) Answer: A

Elise = Mia – 8 ⇒ Mia = Elise + 8

Elise = Mason – 5 ⇒ Mason = Elise + 5

Mia + Elise + Mason = 61

Now, replace the ages of Mia and Mason by Elise. Then:

Elise + 8 + Elise + Elise + 5 = 61

3Elise + 13 = 61   ⇒ 3Elise = 61 – 13

3Elise = 48 ⇒ Elise = 16

2) Answer: D

$$distance = speed \times time \Rightarrow time = \frac{distance}{speed} = \frac{540+540}{18} = 60$$

(Round trip means that the distance is 1,080 miles)

The round trip takes 60 hours. Change hours to minutes, then:

$60 \times 60 = 3,600$

3) Answer: D

Change 7 hours to minutes, then: $7 \times 60 = 420$ minutes

$\frac{420}{70} = 6$

4) Answer: B

Since Julie gives 9 pieces of candy to each of her friends, then, then number of pieces of candies must be divisible by 9.

A. $168 \div 9 = 18.66$

B. $738 \div 9 = 82$

C. $856 \div 9 = 95.11$

D. $472 \div 9 = 52.44$

Only choice B gives a whole number.

5) Answer: B

Area of a rectangle = width × length = $30 \times 48 = 1,440$

6) Answer: C

$$average = \frac{sum}{total}$$

Sum = $4 + 6 + 21 + 30 + 22 + 31 = 114$

Total number of numbers = 6

$$average = \frac{114}{6} = 19$$

7) Answer: D

The base rate is $18.

The fee for the first 40 visits is: $40 \times 0.35 = 14$

The fee for the visits 41 to 50 is: $10 \times 0.3 = 3$

Total charge: $18 + 14 + 3 = 35$

8) Answer: A

$$average = \frac{sum}{total} = \frac{53+57+40}{3} = \frac{150}{3} = 50$$

9) Answer: B

Find the value of each choice:

A. $2 \times 3 \times 3 \times 5 = 90$

B. $2 \times 2 \times 2 \times 3 \times 3 \times 5 = 360$

C. $3 \times 7 = 21$

D. $2 \times 3 \times 3 \times 7 = 126$

10) Answer: B

The amount they have = $18.47 + $28.25 + $31.12 = 77.84$

11) Answer: C

21 dozen of magazines are 252 magazines: $21 \times 12 = 252$

$252 - 76 = 176$

12) Answer: B

$$Probability = \frac{desired\ outcomes}{possible\ outcomes} = \frac{8}{8+7+14+19} = \frac{8}{48} = \frac{1}{6}$$

13) Answer: B

1 ton = 2,000 pounds

9 ton = 18,000 pounds

$\frac{54,000}{18,000} = 3$

William needs to make at least 3 trips to deliver all the food.

14) Answer: C

$220 - 60 - 90 = 70$

15) Answer: D

Each worker can walk 3 dogs: $9 \div 3 = 3$

4 workers can walk 12 dogs. $4 \times 3 = 12$

16) Answer: D

$36 \div 6 = 6$ hours for one course

$6 \times 25 = 150 \Rightarrow \$150$

Practice Test 1 - CAT

Mathematics Knowledge

1) Answer: C

Only choice C is not equal to 7^2

2) Answer: D

If a = 9 then:

$b = \frac{a^2}{3} + 2 \Rightarrow b = \frac{9^2}{3} + 2 = 27 + 2 = 29$

3) Answer: C

$\sqrt[6]{64} = 2$

$(2^6 = 2 \times 2 \times 2 \times 2 \times 2 \times 2 = 64)$

4) Answer: B

(r = radius): Area of a circle $= \pi r^2 = \pi \times (5)^2 = 3.14 \times 25 = 78.5$

5) Answer: A

$-7a = 63 \Rightarrow a = \frac{63}{-7} = -9$

6) Answer: D

All angles in a triable add up to 180 degrees.

$90° + 52° = 142°$

$x = 180° - 142° = 38°$

7) Answer: B

In scientific notation form, numbers are written with one whole number times 10 to the power of a whole number. Number 826,470 has 6 digits. Write the number and after the first digit put the decimal point. Then, multiply the number by 10 to the power of 5 (number of remaining digits). Then:

$826,470 = 8.2647 \times 10^5$

8) Answer: C

Use Pythagorean Theorem: $a^2 + b^2 = c^2$

$(6)^2 + (8)^2 = c^2 \quad \Rightarrow \quad 36 + 64 = 100 = C^2 \Rightarrow C = \sqrt{100} = 10$

9) Answer: C

Use FOIL (first, out, in, last) method.

$(2x + 2)(4x + 3) = 8x^2 + 6x + 8x + 6 = 8x^2 + 14x + 6$

10) Answer: D

$6(a - 3) = 18 \Rightarrow 6a - 18 = 18 \Rightarrow 6a = 18 + 18 = 36$

$\Rightarrow 6a = 36 \Rightarrow a = \frac{36}{6} = 6$

11) Answer: D

Use exponent multiplication rule:

$x^a \times x^b = x^{a+b}, (x^a)^b = x^{ab}$

Then: $9^{12} = (3^2)^{12} = 3^{24} = 3^9 \times 3^{3x} = 2^{9+3x}$

$24 = 9 + 3x \Rightarrow 3x = 24 - 9 = 15 \Rightarrow x = 5$

12) Answer: A

An obtuse angle is an angle of greater than 90 degrees and less than 180 degrees. Only choice A is an obtuse angle.

13) Answer: C

To factor the expression $x^2 - 6x + 8$, we need to find two numbers whose sum is -6 and their product is 8.

Those numbers are -2 and -4. Then: $x^2 - 6x + 8 = (x - 4)(x - 2)$

14) Answer: B

Slope of a line: $\frac{y_2 - y_1}{x_2 - x_1} = \frac{rise}{run}$

$\frac{y_2 - y_1}{x_2 - x_1} = \frac{8 - 4}{3 - 1} = \frac{4}{2} = 2$

15) Answer: C

$\sqrt{144} = 12$

$\sqrt{36} = 6$

$12 \times 6 = 72$

16) Answer: B

$\sqrt[3]{343} = 7$

Answers and Explanations

Practice Test 2 - Paper and Pencil

Arithmetic Reasoning

1) Answer: D

$$40\% \times 60 = \frac{40}{100} \times 60 = 24$$

The coupon has $24 value. Then, the selling price of the sweater is $36.

$$60 - 24 = 36$$

Add 8% tax, then: $\frac{8}{100} \times 36 = 2.88$ for tax

$$36 + 2.88 = 38.88$$

2) Answer: B

4 weeks = 24 days

Then: $24 \times 2 = 48$ hours

$48 \times 60 = 2,880$ minutes

3) Answer: B

distance= $speed \times time \Rightarrow$ time $= \frac{distance}{speed} = \frac{240+240}{40} = 12$

(Round trip means that the distance is 480 miles)

The round trip takes 12 hours. Change hours to minutes, then:

$$12 \times 60 = 720$$

4) Answer: B

$80 - 28 = 52$ male students

$$\frac{52}{80} = 0.65$$

Change 0.65 to percent $\Rightarrow 0.65 \times 100 = 65\%$

5) Answer: D

The factors of 24 are: $\{1, 2, 3, 4, 6, 8, 12, 24\}$

14, is not a factor of 24.

6) Answer: C

$$average = \frac{sum}{total},$$

Sum = 6 + 10 + 25 + 22+ 18 + 21 = 102

Total number of numbers = 6

$\frac{102}{6} = 17$

7) Answer: A

Emma's three best times are 43, 37, and 46.

The average of these numbers is: $average = \frac{sum}{total}$,

Sum = 43 + 37 + 46 = 126

Total number of numbers = 3

$average = \frac{126}{3} = 42.$

8) Answer: A

The area of 13 feet by 13 feet room is 169 square feet.

13 × 13 = 169

9) Answer: D

3.852369 × 100,000 = 385236.9

10) Answer: D

5 percent of 20 is: $20 \times \frac{5}{100} = 1$

Emma's new rate is 26.

20 + 1 = 21.

11) Answer: A

Emily = Lucas

Emily = 6 Mia   ⇒ Lucas = 6 Mia

Lucas = Mia + 30

then: Lucas = Mia + 30   ⇒ 6Mia = Mia + 30

Remove 1 Mia from both sides of the equation. Then:

5Mia = 30 ⇒ Mia = 6

12) Answer: D

$3^6 = 3 \times 3 \times 3 \times 3 \times 3 \times 3 = 729$

13) Answer: C

Sum $= 20 + 31 + 27 + 42 + 25 = 145$

$average = \dfrac{145}{5} = 29$

14) Answer: C

Perimeter of a rectangle $= 2 \times$ length $+ 2 \times$ width $=$

$2 \times 51 + 2 \times 43 = 102 + 86 = 188$

15) Answer: B

$Speed = \dfrac{\text{distance}}{\text{time}}$

$23.5 = \dfrac{distance}{3.4} \Rightarrow distance = 23.5 \times 3.4 = 79.9$

Rounded to a whole number, the answer is 80.

16) Answer: B

Let's review the choices provided and find their sum.

A. $15 \times 7 = 105$

B. $25 \times 7 = 175 \Rightarrow$ is greater than 150 and less than 200

C. $18 \times 7 = 126$

D. $38 \times 7 = 266$

Only choice B gives a number that is greater than 150 and less than 200.

17) Answer: C

$\dfrac{1 \, hour}{19 \, coffees} = \dfrac{x}{1,900} \Rightarrow 19 \times x = 1 \times 1,900 \Rightarrow 19x = 1,900 \Rightarrow x = 100$

It takes 100 hours until she's made 1,900 coffees.

18) Answer: C

$percent \ of \ change = \dfrac{change}{original \ number},$

$6.68 - 6.30 = 0.38$

$percent \ of \ change = \dfrac{0.38}{6.30} = 0.0603 \Rightarrow 0.0603 \times 100 = 6.03\%$

19) Answer: A

Write a proportion and solve.

$$\frac{\frac{1}{4}inches}{4.25} = \frac{1\ mile}{x}.$$

Use cross multiplication, then: $\frac{1}{4}x = 4.25 \rightarrow x = 17$.

20) Answer: C

Two candy bars costs 70¢ and a package of peanuts cost 50¢ and a can of cola costs 30¢. The total cost is:

$70 + 50 + 30 = 150$, 150 is equal to 5 quarters. $5 \times 30 = 150$

21) Answer: A

$150 \div 50 = 3$

22) Answer: C

1 quart = 0.25 gallon

42 quarts = $42 \times 0.25 = 10.5$ gallons. then: $\frac{10.5}{3} = 3.5$ weeks

23) Answer: B

The difference of the file added, and the file deleted is:

$867,234 - 758,748 = 108,486$

$752,135 + 108,486 = 860,621$

24) Answer: C

$5y + 7y + 6y = -108 \Rightarrow 18y = -108 \Rightarrow y = -\frac{108}{18} \Rightarrow y = -6$

25) Answer: A

Every day the hour hand of a watch makes 2 complete rotation. ($\frac{360}{30} = 12$) Thus, it makes 14 complete rotations in days. $8 \times 2 = 16$

26) Answer: B

$\sqrt{64} \times \sqrt{25} = 8 \times 5 = 40$

27) Answer: B

$3\frac{4}{15} - 2\frac{2}{5} = 3\frac{4}{15} - 2\frac{6}{15} = 2\frac{19}{15} - 2\frac{6}{15} = \frac{13}{15}$

28) Answer: B

$191 - 23 = 168 ; \frac{168}{14} = 12.$

29) Answer: C

To convert a decimal to percent, multiply it by 100 and then add percent sign (%).

$0.092 \times 100 = 9.20\%$

30) Answer: A

$8x - 11x + 3x = -27 \Rightarrow 0 \neq -27 \Rightarrow$ The equation not related to x and you can choose

any number.

Practice Test 2 - Paper and Pencil

Mathematics Knowledge

1) Answer: B

$5(3x^5)^3 \Rightarrow 5 \times 3^3 \times x^{15} = 135x^{15}$

2) Answer: D

Perimeter of a triangle = side 1 + side 2 + side 3 = 17 + 17 + 17 = 51

3) Answer: C

From the choices provided, 24, 30 and 36 are divisible by 6. From these numbers, 36 is the biggest.

4) Answer: D

Use FOIL (First, Out, In, Last) method.

$(x + 8)(x + 2) = x^2 + 2x + 8x + 16 = x^2 + 10x + 16$

5) Answer: A

In scientific notation form, numbers are written with one whole number times 10 to the power of a whole number. Number 820,000 has 6 digits. Write the number and after the first digit put the decimal point. Then, multiply the number by 10 to the power of 5 (number of remaining digits). Then: $820,000 = 8.2 \times 10^5$

6) Answer: C

An obtuse angle is an angle of greater than 90° and less than 180°.

7) Answer: D

Use exponent multiplication rule: $x^a . x^b = x^{a+b}$

Then: $7^8 \times 7^7 = 7^{15}$

8) Answer: B

4,789.56126 rounded to the nearest tenth equals 4,789.6

(Because 4,789.56 is closer to 4,789.6 than 4,789.5)

9) Answer: A

$\sqrt[3]{729} = 9$

10) Answer: B

Diameter = 16; then: Radius = 8

Area of a circle $= \pi r^2 \Rightarrow A = 3.14(8)^2 = 200.96$

11) Answer: C

Oven 1 = 6 oven 2

Oven 1 + oven 2 = 7 burn pizzas. $161 \div 7 = 23$ oven 2

$161 - 23 = 138$ (6×23) oven 1

12) Answer: A

$n! = n(n-1)(n-2)(n-3)(n-4)!$

$7! = 7 \times 6 \times 5 \times 4! =$

13) Answer: B

Let's review the choices provided. Put the values of x and y in the equation.

A. (2, 6) $\Rightarrow x = 2 \Rightarrow y = 6$ This is true!

B. (−2, −10) $\Rightarrow x = -2 \Rightarrow y = -14$ This is not true!

C. (4, 16) $\Rightarrow x = 4 \Rightarrow y = 16$ This is true!

D. (−1, −9) $\Rightarrow x = -1 \Rightarrow y = -9$ This is true!

14) Answer: D

$5 - (-4) = 9$

15) Answer: D

Use distance formula:

$$d = \sqrt{(x_1 - x_2)^2 + (y_1 - y_2)^2} = \sqrt{(4 - (-1))^2 + (5 - (-7))^2}$$

$$\sqrt{25 + 144} = \sqrt{169} = 13$$

16) Answer: A

$x^2 - 49 = 0 \Rightarrow x^2 = 49 \Rightarrow x$ could be 7 or −7

17) Answer: A

Area of a rectangle = width × length = $110 \times 140 = 15,400$

18) Answer: D

factor of 112 = {1, 2, 4, 7, 8, 14, 16, 28, 56, 112}. 9 is not a factor of 112.

19) Answer: C

Let's review the choices provided.

A. $45 \times 4 = 180$

B. $60 \times 4 = 240$

C. $38 \times 4 = 152$

D. $52 \times 4 = 208$

From choices provided, only 152 is greater than 110 and less than 160.

20) Answer: C

The cube of $10 = 10 \times 10 \times 10 = 1,000$

$\frac{1}{5} \times 1,000 = 200$

21) Answer: D

From the list of numbers, 13, 7, and 23 are prime numbers. Their sum is:

$13 + 7 + 23 = 43$

22) Answer: C

$30\% = \frac{30}{100} = \frac{3}{10}$

23) Answer: C

Number 8.54869 should be multiplied by 1,000 in order to obtain the number 8,548.69

$8.54869 \times 1,000 = 8,548.69$

24) Answer: B

Two Angles are supplementary when they add up to 180 degrees.

$115° + 65° = 180°$

25) Answer: C

$\frac{25}{100} \times 80 = 20$

"End"